MAMMONOCRACY

THE GOVERNMENT OF MONEY, BY MONEY, FOR MONEY

MAMMONOCRACY

THE GOVERNMENT OF MONEY, BY MONEY, FOR MONEY

A SIMPLE PERSON'S GUIDE BY

CHRISTOPHER WEARNE

New Generation Publishing

Contents

1

What is There to Grumble About?

Money isn't everything. It's just most everything.

Nica Clark

20 years ago the average CEO of a FTSE company earned 25 times the average worker's wage; today the multiple is close to 100 times.

Will Hutton in the Guardian,
January 2007

Money doesn't sleep.

Anonymous

Money begets money.

John Ray
(1627–1705)

The point is that you can't be too greedy.

Donald Trump

Will anyone halt the rise of Britain's super-rich?

Headline in the Independent,
September 2007

So, here is the question. Is the country a success story or is the country grinding to a halt? Pick your own examples from these: riots and protests, record profits, an obesity crisis, skill shortages, best ever A-level results, overloaded A & E services, record house prices in London, property out of reach for workers with essential skills, cheap holidays abroad, record levels of stress at the workplace…

There are two separate little worlds out there; what follows is a simple attempt to explain the common cause.

THE NEGATIVE VIEW

First, start with a slightly silly book… *Is it Just Me or is Everything Shit?* A country that is at ease with itself could never spawn such demand for this book. Too much that doesn't work well any more? Disputes over pensions, milk and fuel prices; aren't they all just symptoms of insufficient income over a variety of sectors? Is there not a serious problem when 25,000 police go on a protest march and nurses talk openly of strikes?

Why? Market forces? Too much hassle, and not enough money in the business any more. Schools? Why are good teachers in short supply? Too much hassle and not enough money. Nurses and police – the same. Manufacturing and engineering? Struggling to stay in business. Farming? Selling up. What is the common thread? These are people trying to do something for a living, to generate wealth, or assist those who do so.

THE POSITIVE VIEW

Now look at the other view of Britain. Low inflation, and compared to parts of the Eurozone, low unemployment; shares are still relatively buoyant. We have avoided a lot of trouble by staying out of the Euro and we still see many Britons travelling abroad for holidays or for weekends away in foreign cities. Surely, there should not be a problem. Those who control our business affairs see no need for fundamental change.

THE TWO VIEWS IN HARMONY?

So, which is the true picture? Gloom or boom? The answer is both, but the answer is also very simple. As others have started to notice, there are two economies. The first element we shall crudely refer to as Wealth Generation, the second we shall call Wealth Control.

The first half, Wealth Generation, is very easy to understand. Generating production and the means of production, assisting and developing, repairing people and the means of production. Do we not see a strain on every moving part – hospitals, schools, factories, and the countryside?

Now let's have a look at Wealth Control. Is this where we find the satisfied silence of share options, tax advisors and imported cars? There has always been a need for Wealth Control, as an adjunct to Wealth Generation, a grouping that controls much of the economy. This has grown bigger, its processes more extensive; more middlemen between production and those who would buy the fruits of that production. These sectors are certainly in far, far better shape than the productive ones and their direct support.

THE TWIN TRACK ECONOMY

So there is the twin track economy. And how do we know that Wealth Control are in control? Ask the basic questions. Which sector has got rich as other sectors have got poorer? Who benefits when industries are sold abroad or privatised? Who benefitted most as the cost of the legal system rose and rose? Which grouping has controlled everybody's cost bar their own? Yet it is a grouping that generates little real wealth. Ladies and gentlemen, meet Wealth Control; in simple terms, they are the present management team for GB plc.

THE TWIN TRACKS ON COLLISION COURSE

And where do the police protests, tuition fees and the uncertainty surrounding the NHS fit into all this? Isn't it the case that those protesters are in the same bind as broke farmers, overstressed technicians, tired teachers, and insecure short-term workers? Their struggle is of those whose function is fundamentally productive – Wealth Generation – to lessen the burden imposed on them by those whose function is fundamentally parasitic – Wealth Control.

INTRODUCING THE CONCEPT OF MAMMONOCRACY

The comments above suggest that GB plc should be defined as a

Mammonocracy: government by money, of money, for money.

2

So, How Did We Get Here?

Money does not change men, it only unmasks them.

Madame Riccoboni
(1714–1792)

Are investment bankers and other professional advisers such as lawyers and accountants, no more than parasites that live off the hard work of corporations and the hard-earned savings of the Great British Public?

Excerpt from introduction to The Power 100,
a review of the most influential figures in British business,
The Times, January 2008

Capitalism is using its money; we socialists throw it away.

Fidel Castro

This lady's not for turning.

Margaret Thatcher, 1980

T his is intended to be a whistle-stop explanation into the present state of GB plc. Yes, there are over 200 years of social and economic history to consider. If you want to understand all of that, please go and buy a proper economics book; if five minutes will do, read on.

SEVENTIES AND STRIKES

A good starting point is GB plc in about 1975. Remember a country frustrated by strikes – by power workers, miners, firemen and throughout manufacturing. Think of TUC 'card' votes, where a single conference delegate could hold a card that entitled him to vote for 1,400,000 people; Denis Healey turning round to address domestic financial crises when bound for Paris; print workers defending the right for payment for being largely superfluous at work; Red Robbo; Arthur Slagheap. It could not last, and it did not. For a time, control of the economy was mainly with those who controlled the means to production. If the attitude of any one grouping of people made Mrs Thatcher possible, it was these. 1979 brought the Winter of Discontent. It crystallised opinion against this point of control. A government that sought accommodation with this point of control was dumped in favour of one that undertook to attack it head on. Enter the Iron Lady.

MRS THATCHER AND HER ALLIES

'…where there is discord, let there be harmony…'

Nobody laughed as Mrs T intoned St Francis' words; not only did she mean it, she had wide public support. Her electoral success was the first of three points of control: politics, economy and law.

Next, we should remember the first theoretical plank of her

economic policy: monetarism. The simple premise was that if you constricted the supply of money, through high borrowing costs and restricted public spending, inflation would be cured. It was an incredibly crude method but it fulfilled its one aim. As a means of controlling the economy, monetarism was as subtle as running amok with buzz saws in a forest; many of the trees that survived had shown resilience and many of those felled were among the weak. At its height the policy caused inflation, but within the target period, in time for a General Election, the policy worked and inflation was under control.

In parallel, legal moves to cement the new control mechanism started. Laws of employment were overhauled, to restrict the extent to which strikes could break out in industry. Of course, once the policy was in place, the government soon found a solid group of commercial allies, ready to assist: Murdoch, Eddy Shah, Ian McGregor and the rest. By 1981 there were riots. By 1982, there was the Falklands and their war. The opposition was Michael Foot and his pump. By 1983 Mrs T was in place for a second term.

MRS THATCHER BUILDS HER EDIFICE

With five more years safely secured, Mrs T continued to develop her policies. By 1984 she was ready for her emblematic battle for control of the economy: the miners' strike. This showed everybody that control of money – a *stick* – could exert greater influence than control of means of production. The policy of privatisation was the *carrot*. There is little doubt that many positive benefits resulted from privatisations. The move brought commercial focus into areas that had become complacent: housing, telephones and aerospace, to name a few. Efficiency could be measured by profits and the demonstrable result was increase in profits – a good result all round, it seemed. Some of the best business brains got to run some of the most worthwhile businesses. 1986 saw the 'Big Bang' ushering in an era of deregulated money markets. By the 1987 election Mrs T had no need for a war or weak opposition; she was no longer quoting St Francis of Assisi, either.

EIGHTIES AND LOADSAMONEY

By 1988, all the groundwork put in place over nine years was bearing fruit, with Nigel Lawson's great giveaway budget. Big bonuses, 'Loadsamoney' and galloping house prices were the great themes. The Conservatives and the pound seemed unsinkable. Policy direction had been set and there seemed little need to alter course: choice, freedoms, more privatisations, lower direct taxes. But is it not true that, by then, the policies themselves were entering the field of diminishing returns? The Government got cocky and introduced the Poll Tax; Tories started to argue with Tories. Time for a change?

IN OFFICE IF NOT IN POWER

By 1991, the Conservatives had decided that electoral success was more important than Mrs T's tired-looking and purist values. John Major was, it has to be said, an inspired choice of replacement. He managed to appear to control the excesses of Thatcherism just enough, just exactly enough, to win the 1992 election and unleash most of those excesses for another five years.

Norman Lamont later complained that the Government were in office but not in power. He was missing the bigger point. Surely, the Government did not have to do much; they did not need to. They had the economy where they wanted it, and all that was to be done was to defend that position. If anything showed the extent of that Government's level of control it was the fact that they managed to privatise the railways. That control was symptomatic of the grip that the forces of Wealth Control had developed.

The Major years showed that Mrs Thatcher's edifice had gained a strength beyond her dreams. In simple terms, the effect was to treat money the same way as any other commodity; by restricting supply, the cost – interest – went up, and the influence of the commodity owners – the rich – was greatly increased.

THE TORY LEGACY

So there it is, a potted history of eighteen years of Conservative rule. But this still does not fully explain the present. For those of you who are new to the subject, believe us, it was not always like this. And, to those of you who were politically aware in 1997, does the country feel radically different now to the way it felt then? Different, yes, but not radically so. Are not many of the fundamental shortcomings still present despite several years of a different political climate?

Strangely, there is an explanation. Surely this is a reflection not only on the Government but on the thoroughness with which the wealth control mechanisms were set up? Not only was eighteen years of dominance achieved but the edifice was so well built that other incoming Governments have not been able, or willing, to greatly change it. By 1997, the control of finance and law was so strong that successive Labour Governments sought not to make changes, but sought instead to accommodate the new model.

INTRODUCING THE CURRENT MANAGEMENT TEAM

The above is a hugely abbreviated introduction to the appointment of the current management team for GB plc. So, be ready for some big generalisations, but come and have a look at the world of Wealth Control.

3

INTRODUCING THE MANAGEMENT AND THEIR CULTURE

Business is the art of extracting money from another man's pocket without resorting to violence.

Max Amsterdam

It is easier for a camel to pass through the eye of a needle than for a rich man to enter the kingdom of God.

Jesus of Nazareth,
Matthew 19:24

Money is the new form of slavery and distinguishes from the old simply by the fact that it is impersonal – that there is no interpersonal relationship between master and slave.

Leo Tolstoy
(1928–1910)

The care of a large estate is an unpleasant thing.

Juvenal
(AD 60–140)

Because management is seen as a good thing in itself, managers feel free to spread it everywhere. Frequently the methods it involves don't work, which mean that more managers are required to force it to work. Managers set wages, and since they rate management highly, managers get the fattest pay packets. This draws more people into management and away from actually doing whatever their organisation is supposed to do.

Simon Hoggart, writing in the *Guardian*,
March 2002

I dentification of the management team of a firm is like identifying the leaders in a team; the evidence is found in various forms. There are the mechanisms, the behaviour of the parties, the priorities set and, of course, the way in which the rewards are divided. First, let's discuss who they are in brief.

THE THREE PILLARS – POLITICS, FINANCE AND PROCESS

We started with politics, so let's look there for the first clues. Gone are the days when MPs complain about pay rates. OK, the hours are ridiculous but the rewards are better than most. And then there are all the Members' interests: directorships, 'expenses', consultancies, etc. Are these people so rewarded because they are brilliant strategists, the crème de la crème, experts in their fields? No, it's because they have influence – influence on the other forces of Wealth Control. There is no wish here to devalue the efforts of many active political people who have no financial interest, but too many seem to have become part of the system. The country now boasts an influential group of professional politicians. George W Bush did not set too many trends, but he started one by appointing a cabinet that read like a Who's Who of US big business. The point is that the two influences – wealth and politics – have, to mutual benefit, become entwined. Ashcroft, Archer, Aitken, Abrahams... that's just the 'A's.

And then look at financial control: at the top there's the Treasury, the civil servants whose main discipline is accountability and financial control, with an increasing involvement of private sector culture. They control the flow of money from the Government. Next to them are the major financial institution heads: banks, investment banks, etc. They control the flow of nearly all the rest of the money in the economy. And most of that flow is controlled by the major companies, the plcs, etc. And it is accepted fact that these majors control the way business is done in the rest of the economy. Add in the politicisation of the Civil Service and the tightening of the bonds between these groups, and there is the control from the top down.

In parallel with the finance groups there is the legal system. This operates in precisely the same way, with the control being traceable from the top down. If the money men pull the strings, the legal people represent the strings themselves. What is significant is the limited extent to which anyone else can influence events these days without reference to financial or legal expertise. Try – you won't get very far.

So, those are the people with their collective role and identity: Wealth Control. 'Wealth' here means more than mere cash; it means money supply, property, assets, anything that can generate future wealth. Parallels have been drawn between mature capitalism and the Roman Empire; their control was politics, army, finance; the modern equivalents are politics, process, finance. Their control is visible in so many ways – mechanisms, behaviours, priorities and the division of the rewards.

THE MECHANISM – COMPETITION

It is instructive to note that all the way through the development of Mrs T's central policies one policy goal remained constant: competition. It was applied wherever she chose; the market was always deemed to be right. What is most interesting is that this was applied to all areas except those which Mrs T found were helpful to her. Politics and finance became entangled to mutual benefit. QCs were not made to compete with each other within a fixed budget, nor were accountants. The harsh, real competition is further down the wealth equivalent of the food chain: for jobs, for opportunities, for orders; for cockle-pickers, waiters, twenty-four-hour shop staff, and the rest.

HOW THE SYSTEM PROTECTS THE RULING CLASS

To look at behaviours, take a slightly silly example, but one with a grain of truth in it. How many qualified staff does it take to change a light bulb? Well, first, the legal team ought to check that it's not someone else's to change. Then the finance team will need to set up orders etc. to 'capture the costs' etc. And changing the light bulb? Ah, the light bulb… The management don't much care who does that, as long as there's a risk assessment and it's done cheaply. So where does the money go? More to the group who administer the whole process, and proportionally less for the poor electrician; and, of course, the ruling class earn a percentage of the now increased financial turnover.

Everyone accepts that money is tight around most of GB plc, but it appears necessary for each little local transaction to be sanctioned by local treasurers and their managers or department heads. There's not much empowerment or trust. These people then justify their actions to the banks, and they in turn justify their actions to this elite group of people at the top: control within control. The needs arise from the bottom up and many a business plan has been sought from managers with the instruction 'from the bottom up'. But we all know that the important decision – yes or no – comes from the top down.

PRIORITIES – CASH IS KING

And then there is the great saw that 'cash is king'. Look at the national and public services, the NHS, the railways, schools. The same processes have been applied. Is Network Rail run by a Chartered Engineer or the NHS by a doctor? And it is reflected in the values under which they are run: reduced costs, efficiency, and financial control. There are instances where it all seems like a great experiment, to see how much expenditure can be removed from the service before it fails to function properly. NHS supremos talk of targets and levels of expenditure, but hospitals do not reflect this shining vision. Company annual reports are full of self-congratulatory references, but the service users don't always see it the same way. The reality is that a smaller, cash-starved workforce can make things work, but not as well and not as thoroughly; items slip through the net such as BSE, Shipman, Baby 'P' and the unfortunately named *Herald of Free Enterprise*.

There is another reason why senior people like to say that cash is king. They have the cash. The cash makes them powerful.

RESULTS AND REWARDS

And finally there are the rewards. Look at our three pillars. Have we heard about jobless lawyers, barristers on their uppers, accountants trading down or bankers going bankrupt? Not much of that about, is there? And aren't there are a lot of politicians living in impressive houses? Who had heard of Max Clifford and all those publicists twenty-five years ago? We hear from ICAEW's Career Benchmarking Survey that the *average* salary for chartered accountants is £79.4k, from a report published in June 2007. That is a very healthy average. Then we can look at the people who do the work by looking at a typical municipal public service. Twenty years ago it probably employed a large group of local people and was run by experienced operators in their fields. And now? The workforce are rushed, stressed and insecure. And where did the savings go? On other services? Reduced costs to the taxpayer? Where then? If the management wanted to tell us they would. The fact that they don't suggests they have done rather well out of the arrangements they have put in place.

4

Introducing a New Middle Class – Management Support

Do I hear you offering the drug companies' time-worn excuse that they need to make huge profits on one drug to finance the development of others? Then kindly tell me, please, how they spend twice as much on marketing as they do on research and development?

John Le Carre,
The Nation, 2001

It may well be that the various forms of monitoring, assessment and data collection are intended to make things better, but this is far from obvious to many of those who actually have to wade through the needless paperwork. Indeed, the practical benefit of this kind of academic bureaucracy is almost impossible to discern, and it is hard to avoid the suspicion that its main aim is to reduce the complexities of teaching and research to data to be crunched in the service of a government promoting the appearance of fostering decentralisation and autonomy; while, in fact, centralising control.

Letter to the Guardian,
Charlie Gere, December 2006

We spend around £38 per head on legal aid annually in England and Wales, compared to £4 in Germany and £3 in France.

Lord Hunt, Parliamentary undersecretary
of state in the Ministry of Justice, January 2008

The problem of our age is the proper administration of wealth, so that the ties of brotherhood may still bind together the rich and poor in harmonious relationship.

Andrew Carnegie
(1835–1919)

So, we have discussed Wealth Control, the ruling class. Now, what about the rest of society? Now, we know a bit about the working class and who they are, but there is something else here. There is a group that has become most significant. It is those who assist Wealth Control. We are aware that they are there and vaguely aware of them as a burden, but we have never really defined them.

What do they do? They do not make many of the rules and therefore they are not part of the ruling class. They are not people who carry out the real jobs that make the world go round; they are not of the working class. They are in between these two groups, in the middle.

If the ruling class define the rules for transactions and the working class carry out the productive tasks, we need a definition for those who occupy the middle. Let us call them Management Support. They are the new middle class.

Their roles can be better understood by looking at them in the light of the three ruling groups of politics, process and finance.

MANAGEMENT SUPPORT IN POLITICS AND PROPAGANDA

The first part of the structure can be seen in the appropriation of the administrative machinery. We all know that statisticians can prove anything. The management know that and use it. For an example, each public organisation now has to provide great swathes of statistics for compiling performance tables. It is the same for schools, police forces and the rest. Someone somewhere must have a huge bank of figures or a disc 'in the post' to tell us that hospital waiting lists are longer, shorter or whatever. Presumably, as an aside, if these undoubtedly capable people were actively contributing to the cause, the results would be better. Presumably also, the fact that the improvement would not be demonstrated would means that this is no use to the management, so it will not happen. These people are capable of contributing productively, but the management prefers to have them as support.

Of course the same logic dictates that each organisation must produce a 'mission statement'. St Thomas' Hospital boasts that it is 'Serving the Community 24 hours a day'. Why does it need to deny an intent to do anything else? To serve from nine to five, and after that you can go hang? To serve the managers, and the rest can lump it? Actually, the clue is in the title – it is a *hospital*. Obvious, you might think. It is slightly redolent of the German Democratic Republic and the Democratic People's Republic of North Korea – those beacons of human fulfilment.

MANAGEMENT SUPPORT IN PROCESS AND PROCEDURES

The administrative machinery also uses huge amounts of resources to set up procedures. The legal profession, for example, does well here: witness the extensive procedural checks required merely to arrest a red-handed felon, or the tendency for lawyers to gather round and have a long discussion, at the expense of others. In 2007 Labour's Lord Hunt's confirmation that we spend £38 pa per head on legal aid in England and Wales, compared to £4 in Germany and £3 in France was intended as good news. But, in a competitive global market-place this sounds anything but good news.

Another group within Management Support consists of those who devise protocols for preventing complaining customers reaching anyone remotely able to offer a human response. This element appears specifically employed to protect the working, productive person from a demand of time from a real living client. So, if you can stumble through the door and remember your name, you can get several thousand pounds' worth of credit on the high street. But if it goes wrong you will need a diploma in project management to get your money back, through a labyrinth devised by Management Support staff.

MANAGEMENT SUPPORT IN FINANCE

This is the most obvious role of Management Support and one which has always existed. There is nothing new here. The aspect that is new is the power these people wield. Gone are the days when work starts on the basis that 'an order will follow later'. The transaction must be set up first. And who holds the power in this situation? Management Support.

THE ROLE OF INFORMATION TECHNOLOGY

Older readers will remember promises about how computers would make our lives so much easier. Does the reality feel like that? Not really. Frequently, we hear of another government IT scheme that has absorbed a huge budget, but the efficiencies are not noticeable on the ground, in real life.

Doesn't it seem that it has just become easier to assemble massively detailed systems for Management Support? So, the IT giants absorb huge sums of money and what they provide are systems that give the management a huge amount of information about every transaction that we make. But notice how those transactions – booking an appointment, paying at the shop or setting up an order – are little faster than they were. Big Brother is not watching you, but you do have to give an awful lot of information to his computers.

INTRODUCING THE "COMPLICATIONISTS"

Now, let's be fair, no one sets out on a career with an ambition to complicate the lives of others. But, we all know it happens. Also, no one doubts the need for checks and balances, but there are plenty of examples where it seems to have all got a bit out of hand. For a harmless example, we can look at the need for water in an office. There was a time when a simple fountain sufficed. Now we have the station, the cooler, the packaging, the delivery van and the risk assessment for lifting the containers. What's going on? Well, if you have a load of people with degrees who have ambitions to manage something, then you need projects; you need complications.

So then you need project managers to sort it all out. Brilliant: all of this, remember, to transfer Britain's most famous commodity, rain, to those who are thirsty.

And of course, once the Complicationists have a bridgehead on any given shore – CRB checks, safety of charity events, Great Crested Newts, etc. – the complication is next to impossible to shift. It is also someone's job, and they will not readily give it up. Anyone who wants change has to fight for managers' attention, grapple with vested interests and wrestle with risk assessments and the rest. The managers are busy attending meetings, filling in forms and hurtling round complaining of the lack of time to do anything to address the lack of time. The situation is so much a feature of modern life that it deserves a name; we can call it Dynamic Inertia.

THE THREE 'B'S

There is a simple way of remembering who provides Management Support. They cover, broadly, three subjects: bullshit, bureaucracy and bean-counters. They don't sound as impressive now, but they are essential for the ruling class to remain in control. Of course, to a great extent these people are used as a buffer between the real work and the main management group. And by enlisting support in this way, the ruling class have divided the rest of the workforce, which enhances their control.

MANAGEMENT SUPPORT PROVIDED BY THE WORKING CLASS

Another way in which the ruling class have extended influence is through allowing selected members of the working class to have access to management influence; in other words, there are members of the working class who dabble in Wealth Control. Look at GPs. In 2006 they increased their pay by an average 20%. How? By signing up to new targets and producing the paper to show they had done it. They are now part experts, part Management Support. In our class system, they have gone up in the world. It follows that they get more money.

Management Support – why do they do it?

An important facet of all the groupings noted above is that as groupings they hold a lot of power. It could be argued that as a group they have sold out. That seems harsh; they have been looked after, and because of that, they look after the interest of those who have looked after them. Ask a group of them how they feel about being one of the Three 'B's and you will probably get one of three responses. Some will aspire to become Managers – many find it's dull, comfortable and pays quite well – and most of the rest wish they could go back to doing some real work.

And the rest of the workforce – working class?

Well... yes. We finally come to the remainder: butchers, bakers, candlestick makers, teachers, engineers, secretaries, nurses, farmers, mechanics, drivers, waiters, musicians, call-centre operatives; the people who learn a trade or skill and, by using it, make the world go round. They are the people who do the real Wealth Generation. They are the new working class.

5

Introducing the New Working Class – Wealth Generation

Despite the fact that we have been told that this is an entrepreneurial society, Britain has an utter contempt for skill. If one talks to people who dig coal and drive trains, or to doctors, nurses, dentists or toolmakers, one discovers that no one in Britain is interested in them.

Tony Benn,
1990

Life is work; work is life for the willing slaves who hand over such large chunks of themselves to their employer in return for the pay cheque. The price is heavy in the loss of privacy, the loss of autonomy over the innermost workings of one's emotions, and the compromising of authenticity. The logical conclusion, unless challenged, is capitalism at its most inhuman – the commodification of human beings.

Madeleine Bunting, extract from *Willing Slaves*.

The worker has become as dispensable as Kleenex.

Studs Terkel,
1998

We are treated worse than animals but if we complain we get no work. Our agency breaks the law but nobody seems to care.

Vicktor, food worker, quoted in
'Back the Bill' campaign, February 2008.

Well, we have been through two groups of people, and hardly a stroke of recognisable 'work' has come into view. Finally, we come to the rest: butchers, bakers, candlestick makers and all the other 'doers' mentioned above. Aren't these the people who really make the world go round? They are. Now let us look at their place in the hierarchy.

Look at the people in Wealth Generation. Do they have influence in the wider scheme of things? When a great issue of state arises – ID cards, Iraqi weapons, etc. – does the Government take the view of the experts or the propagandists? Too often it is the latter. When Rover goes bust, does the Government take the view of the workforce or the administrators? It is, again, the latter. So artisans and experts, veterinary scientists and welders are in the same group. They have little control over their work, less influence and, due to the influence of competition, get less money for it than you might expect. Welcome, Professor, to the new working class, a class working under conditions devised by Management Support, which itself is working for the ruling class that is Wealth Control.

THE APPLICATION OF 'COMPETITION' – DIVIDE AND RULE

We have already discussed how the principle has been applied selectively and how the effects reflect the revised class system. Judges are not made to compete with each other within a fixed budget, nor are accountants. The privatised utilities have regulation, not competition. There is competition in big business but much of it comfortable and profitable – supermarkets, breweries, the oil giants. We have already seen where the harsh, real competition is: further down the wealth equivalent of the food chain, for jobs, for opportunities, for orders. And what is this competition? It is not just others in a location who share a specific skill; competition comes from Eastern European skilled workers, from Chinese toy factories and from machines. The competition is harsh and it is everywhere – harvesting winter vegetables, waiting on tables and at the checkouts. As an example of the way this operates look at suppliers who supply the supermarkets, mostly on short-term contracts, to allow scope for a lower price to be obtained next time. For contractors to provide public services, the same logic applies, on limited term contracts again.

The management are in charge of the competition, Management Support help them run it and the rest are in the competition, from Robbie Williams, through the professional skill groups to the skilled workers and the rest. Wealth Generators get paid according to the workings of a market, some much more than the others, but the important thing is this: others run the market, and those others have the choice of how they run it. To an extent they have set up a Dutch auction, at which the rest of us have to bid low for the right to carry out our daily tasks.

DIVIDE AND RULE – COMPETING SECTORS OF THE NEW WORKING CLASS

We have seen how members of the working class have to compete, but there is a second level to this competition. Many of the sectors are in competition with each other. So, when local government budgets are set, by managers, the education lot, for example, compete with the waste disposal people, the highways group, the leisure services and the regeneration department. And they are all given targets, most of which take no account of the need for joined-up thinking at all. So, after a flood, it is found that planners – having met target times for processing applications – have not always had time to wait for data from the flood modellers – whose targets lie elsewhere – and the lass at the insurers has been told, if in doubt, not to offer cover. No one seems to blame the money men for simply not allowing sufficient resources, and no one blames the managers for setting people against their fellows in the first place. The managers rule and then they divide, and then they set the divided against the divided.

DIVIDE AND RULE – DILUTIONS OF THE POWER OF THE WEALTH GENERATORS

The 'divide and rule' principle is applied through other means as well as competition. Take the example of the hospital staff, who are encouraged to work for commercial clinics, with the incentive of sharing profits; they effectively get more money for diluting the bargaining power of the collective. In science, the commercial considerations determine which areas of research get the money; the best money goes to developing the potentially profitable drugs, thus placing priority on finance rather than results that best benefit society. In industry, many of the best brains are encouraged to sit MBAs, to sharpen their commercial edge rather than develop their specific industrial specialism. At the same time, we invest less on real skills and expertise. Why is there a greater financial reward for a mediocre teacher who can administer a department's affairs than an inspiring class teacher? What a devaluing of skill! None of these tendencies appear significant but they add up to a convenient dilution of opposition to the principles of Wealth Control. Go back to GPs and their pay rise. In each of these cases, Wealth Control has paid extra for a few members – 'divide and rule' – of the working class to contribute to the Management Support function and the work of the ruling class.

THE NEW AGENDA FOR WEALTH GENERATORS – AS SET BY MANAGEMENT SUPPORT

Following a 2004 survey by the Home Office it was concluded that police officers, on average, spent only half of their time on front-line duties, the rest being taken up with paperwork. No wonder a Chancellor can boast that spending on the police is higher than ever, and the statistics tell us that crime rates are still too high. Apply the same to teachers – look at all those reports and checks… It even applies to the bloke who cleans the loos at Hilton Park services on the M6. He used to just keep them clean; now he has to sign a card each time, each room, every hour.

There are two points here. First is the fantastic level of waste. Wouldn't it be good to see up to twice as many coppers? But more insidious is the feeling that *doing a job is no longer enough*. You have to wade through a pile of procedure just to prove your value to the great administrative machinery. Someone once said, 'If I did all the things that I ought to do, I'd never get anything done.' PC Plod, among many others, probably shares the view.

THE DEVALUING OF SKILL, EXPERTISE AND SERVICE

In the scenarios noted above it is natural that the expert is left feeling undervalued, marginalised, pressurised and even victimised. This certainly appears to occur more to the British working class – as we have defined them – than to their counterparts in other countries. Our musicians, academics, medics, engineers and designers may be leaders in their fields, but they do not set policy; usually they are just asked to implement it.

6

INTRODUCING THE FORGOTTEN CLASS – DEPENDANTS

What is important to people is to be able to do and be.

Sudhir Anand, Professor of Economics, Oxford University,
describing Amartya Sen's approach to well-being, January 2001

Hundreds of thousands of older people live in poverty due to poor pensions and high taxation.

Campaign literature,
Help The Aged, April 2008

Billions spent, waiting lists increase.

Front headline, *Daily Mail*,
March 2008

My mother waited the statutory four hours on a trolley in A&E, but there was only one doctor on duty.

Sue Arnold, *Independent*,
April 2006

The true measure of a nation's standing is how well it attends to its children – their health and safety, their material security, their education and socialisation and their sense of bring loved, valued and included in the families and societies into which they are born.

From the preface to a 2007 UNICEF report:
'An overview of child well-being in developed countries'.
Britain was ranked twenty-first out of the twenty-one
economically advanced nations that were assessed.

$\mathbf{A}$nd finally, after considering the management structure, its support and the people who carry out the real jobs that make the world go round, we come to the group we forget: Dependants. Yes, we probably think here of the uninvolved, the disenfranchised, the dropouts and those who have decided that they don't wish to contribute at all. But what about the quarter of the population who aren't old enough to work, and the one in seven at the other end of the scale – the retired? It seems natural to discuss this grouping at the end; of course, it should not be so, as they are probably the biggest group of the lot.

Let's start with that observation, that they follow naturally at the tail end of the discussion. This appears natural because this grouping finds itself, in a Mammonocracy, at the end of the food chain. So, as we have noted before, Wealth Control have judged exactly how much ground to give each element of the other classes in order to maintain their control. Dependants, despite being the most populous, have very little influence. Why? They have no job with which to generate the income which provides leverage with the ruling class. Actually, this is just the start of the injustices; let's run through a breakdown of Dependants and take note of some more.

THE YOUNG

Ask yourself a question. Whose work, in the future, is going to pay for the pensions of those of you who are working now? The young. And to what extent are we looking after them at present? TV, lazy food, absent or distracted parents, lack of attention or at least not as much as we might hope. There is no attempt here to enter the debate about who carries out the parental duties, because that does not matter. What *does* matter is the level of commitment to the discipline of parenting at all. That, surely, is what children need if they are to feel as if they are valued. And how is a child meant to feel valued if a parent is more interested in an 'important meeting at work' or a long shift than in being there at bedtime? The child sees the here and now, and 'maybe tomorrow' just feels like plain 'no' to them. To use a child's words, 'downstairs is far'. If the statistics show that 10% of children feel no connection with the society in which they are raised, is it surprising? No. The surprise actually is that the other 90% still do feel connected, still interested in people – their parents – many of whom display relatively little interest in them.

THE UNEMPLOYED

Twenty years ago, this would have been a longer section. If there is one effect of Mammonocracy that has won praise it is the reduction in unemployment. There is a facile explanation for all this employment; it takes a lot of people to milk an economy for all it is worth, as if there is no tomorrow. Credit is due here. Britain, for all its current faults, is a vibrant and busy society. There are also more and more very poorly paid jobs. The bigger concern is whether it is sustainable.

The question here is, the spending years having run their course, how do we look now? Have we used the opportunity to invest in skills and training? No, we are the worst in Europe, preferring to import key workers rather than train. Are we investing in infrastructure to make ourselves more efficient? Well yes, up to a point, but a great deal of the present spend is only addressing a backlog. Visit continental Europe and compare our transport links; even HS2 represents nothing more than catching up.

THE DISABLED

If you really want to see a sector of society that reflects the malevolence of the ruling class and the burden of the Three 'B's, look at disabled care. Most accounts of life in this sector will refer to the suffocation of proactivity by rules and guidelines, many of which appear to protect management as much as the disabled.

The Government's attitude to the Disabled is shown by one recent decision. Remploy is now reducing its workforce. Why? Because of financial pressures – none of the factories break even.

So what? Is it the case that the lack of a profit to keep the bean-counters happy is more important than providing the most essential piece of their identity to several thousand disabled people?

THE OLD

It has often been said that the grey market now has a power it has never had before. There are two reasons: there are a large number of retired people who have considerable wealth; also, there are an unparalleled number of retired people – 13.5% of the population.

Actually, it is quite easy to focus on the wealthy retired: their behaviours are more in tune with those of the ruling class; they have money and therefore influence. They need to be regarded as a part, albeit unwitting, of the ruling class. Although the rest are much more numerous, their voices are rarely heard. Many of them put a huge effort into the War and post-war austerity efforts. Their reward? A state pension scheme that is largely discredited, puny allowances for heating in cold weather, and a tax regime that is better at exploiting the thrift of such people rather than rewarding them.

THE ILL

For those of us in paid employment, illness is the one time that we encounter the lifestyle of Dependants. Illness makes us Dependants. Isn't it a slightly sick society that asks the ill to pay to park at hospital? Then, when you get there you are put on waiting lists for the treatment and made to wait again for, say, the physiotherapist who can help you help yourself to recover. And, if you want to find a decent crowd of medically trained personnel, don't look in a ward, look next to a work station. To an extent, the waiting and the huddle at the PC are two sides of the same coin; the administrative machinery that controls the availability of the care itself. Of course, there is a way of greatly reducing the helplessness of being a Dependant when you are ill. It's called private health care. Which is all right if you can afford it.

Dependants, time and money

Time is money, they say. Life is full of time-versus-money equations. So, Dependants, having little money, have to use great spans of time to get what they want. Look at a bus queue; usually it contains a large proportion of schoolchildren and the elderly. Day centres? No rush here. These people have as valid a need for speedy service as others, but it seems acceptable to offer them otherwise. Why? Because these people have no financial leverage, and in a money-obsessed society, their time is of negligible value. Compare the speed of response to the needs, medical, food, and assistance of CEOs and OAPs. Time and money are interchangeable commodities; Dependants waste huge amounts of time because they have not got the money and are soft targets.

7

LESS MONEY OUT, MORE MONEY IN – WHAT'S THE PROBLEM?

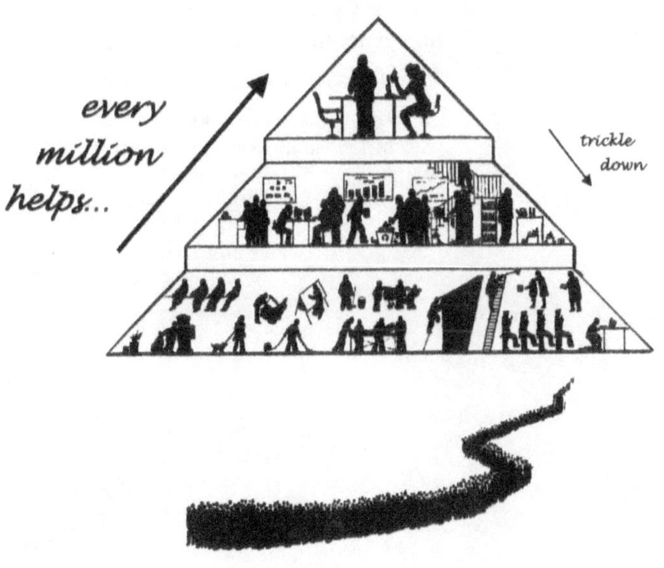

Here is the problem for politicians. It is not reasonable that the most useful body of men should be the worst paid; yet it does not appear that it can be ordered otherwise.

Samuel Johnson
(recorded by James Boswell in 1773)

The cost of privatisation will haunt us for years to come

Headline of article by
Labour MP Kelvin Hopkins in
the *Guardian*, 2006

The private sector will never expose itself to risk unless it is proportionately, if not generously, rewarded. Ultimately, the taxpayer pays the price.

From a report by the House of Commons
Select Transport Committee, January 2008

PFI deals have led to price rises, say MPs

Headline in the *Independent*,
November 2007

I t has been one of successive governments' proudest boasts that Britain is 'competitive', has a 'flexible workforce' and a 'low cost base'. It sounds like a triumph of management, a great benefit to our economy; but is the true picture a little more mixed?

CHOICE AND COMPETITION

Remember the twin aspirations of choice and competition? They were Mrs T's great allies in her vision for Britain. She always wanted to give consumers, customers and buyers of services the greatest choice. Her means for doing this was to set up competition between service providers.

It is useful to follow one of her earliest applications of this: the contracting out of waste disposal services. So, the local authority was forced to ask for tenders from organisations who could do the work. Some authorities tendered themselves, but the usual effect was that the cost to the buyer of the service came down. Some bin men grumbled, some pretty lazy people lost their jobs. So far, so good. The process was expanded, with contracts becoming a bit more sophisticated to avoid low cost equating to low standards. The councils needed a few more contract experts and lawyers but the savings continued to accrue and we all got used to seeing bin men walking at a businesslike pace rather than sauntering. There were grumbles that some council employees would get a redundancy package and then return to the same work next week, with a different pay structure, and reduced pension. And bin men could be seen running... or maybe the lorry was parked in the middle of the road. But it was largely seen as a success.

LESS MONEY OUT – COMPETITION IN ACTION

Then we can look at the application to other sectors. Are there real savings, or are costs just 'externalised' from the accounts? Let's play a game. If taxes have not come down, where have the savings gone?

Take the bin man, who now works for a contractor. He is more efficient, which probably does not hurt him – good – so there is a Cost Saving. But he has got a reduced pension, so he has lost out. That is not Cost Saving any more; that is Cost Avoidance. And we are all being asked to accept fortnightly collections; this represents a Cost Cutting, achieved by a reduction in service.

Now let us move on to one of the more recent policies aimed at Cost Saving – the closure of local post offices. Yes, there are economies of scale which allow a smaller number of staff to provide the same services. But that ignores a crucial fact which is that, in order to reach post offices, customers now have to do much more travelling. That introduces us to Cost Transfer, to the country's infrastructure and the customers themselves. And, when a local post office is closed, no one seems to try to measure the loss of benefit to the community.

Next, an old gripe: the road repair postponed until next year's budget is available. Now, this is messy. The repair is still needed, and may for the delay – no stitches in time – involve a Cost Increase as opposed to Cost Saving. And, surely, really it just puts off the cost – a Cost Deferral. That's not a Cost Saving at all. And the road will cause damage to vehicles, say buses and HGVs; there's a bit of Cost Transfer to others going on here. That sounds like a lose-lose situation.

For another slant, take the hotel business. This would probably collapse without its Eastern European workforce, sweeping, waiting and working in the laundries. Yes, there are major Cost Savings, but ask a local authority Social Services Department for their opinion. They will tell you that the use of imported labour has caused a significant imported liability. The hotels – and we know whom they best serve and to whom they bring most profit – make the Cost Saving, while the boroughs, the LEAs, the local hospital trusts – funded by taxes – pick up the bill. At best it is Cost Avoidance. And there is a nastier subtext here. While Britons have a better attitude to race issues than most, that tolerance will find its limit. Add in the fact that Britain is already a crowded island, and ask whether it helpful in the long term to become more crowded.

Now take a multi-disciplinary contract that goes to an international consortium which uses a multitude of subcontractors and sub-subcontractors and their suppliers? Does anyone check whether all, yes, *all* of the myriad parties have fulfilled all the regulations (remember the unsafe rail hopper that rolled down the hill and killed two men?), have paid UK taxes (as opposed to being registered in Jersey) or have been vetted for reliance on Chinese sweatshops for manufacture? We all know it's going on, and it is worse than Cost Avoidance. That is Cost Evasion.

But we leave the best to last – the PFI contract. Read this slowly, but it goes something like this. A hospital trust or LEA, for example, asks for tenders, from a select list of providers – usually finance backed by construction – to build a brand new facility and operate it for a long period. Competition, yes, except your local builder hardly gets the invite to tender. The client, on behalf of the public, ends up with a defined cost and benefit model. This sounds good, but the client has in fact taken out the equivalent of a huge mortgage. This looks like an enormous Cost Deferral. Now look at that service provider. They start with a guaranteed long-term income stream – the one thing they rarely give to anyone else – and, then, having secured it, are in a strong position to renegotiate terms with both client and their own providers. For organisations devoted to private profit, it's a win-win situation. And Government has found a way of keeping it off the balance sheet: Cost Shoved Under The Carpet. To top it all, the general public hardly appreciates what is going on. Perhaps the public should consider two facts. Most PFI service providers see it as very profitable and lots of hospital trusts are in financial difficulty. Are the two connected?

Now, let's go back to the beginning and revisit the word 'competition'. Who wins? Have we all seen a wondrous lowering of council taxes to pay for public services? Lower income tax because the NHS is cheaper? No. There must be winners somewhere. Each of our examples had losers, generally headed by those doing the real work. But some of the savings are eaten up by the need for consultants and lawyers and contract managers to oversee the competition. And council chief execs are pulling in up to £100k a year. The cost of civil servants goes up. For doing what? Surely, they are largely the combined forces of Wealth Control and Management Support.

And the output of all this organisational effort? To cut the cost. And avoid it, defer it or transfer it to others. To evade it, to show a lower cost and shove a deal of the difference in the pockets of Wealth Control. And, politically, to curb the influence of the Wealth Generators. So, back to the cost-saving benefits of competition... Less Money Out. It looked so clean, but under the microscope, a lot of it is a bit grubby really.

MORE MONEY IN

And what about More Money In? This is easier to explain. In brief, Britain has not been proud about how it increases income. We are kind to Saudi princes who buy hardware from BAe. We accommodate Russian oligarchs with the odd reservation when a Mr Litvinenko dies. Are these folk here for the weather and the culture? Or is it the low taxes and no questions?

Most significantly, London has done very well by being known as the home of the most deregulated financial markets in the world. What about the baffling behaviour of hedge funds, tax breaks for private equity, the emphasis on maximising leverage? Again, we see just enough to worry about the regulation. But is it not only a matter of time before some other financial hub, probably several thousand miles to the East, is more cut-throat, even cheaper, even more deregulated? A worry for the future? It matters rather less if you are a financial deal maker clearing a million each year. But it is a legitimate worry for the rest of us.

Our enthusiasm for income has generated another pressure on our businesses. There is huge pressure – performance bonuses, share options, etc. – that encourage managers to increase turn-over. 125% mortgages and easy credit on the high street, all the way down to bulk-buy discounts, happy hour at the pub and the ubiquitous BOGOF. It is all about turnover – from which the management take their cut of course – and is not always in the best long-term interests of anyone. Repossessed houses, loan sharks, credit crunches and drunks on the streets are the results. Even the mortgage lenders are not immune. The prime example?

Northern Rock. Well, that was the one that appeared first. And the Government intervened because it was rightly scared that there would be a domino-type effect through the banking sector. It could still happen.

The fourth way in which Britain has generated considerable income is from selling off our national assets: airports to the Spanish, for a few billion, of course; water and power to the Germans and French. We are only really world-class at running shops, pharmaceuticals, making things that kill or maim and oiling the wheels of finance. Is it enough?

But put all of these things together and we have wealth today – at long-term cost and risk. What did we learn from Northern Rubble? That earnings and 'value' had been overestimated and risk, liabilities and losses had been underestimated. Now, do we think that the management of GB plc is radically better than that of Northern Rock plc? We shall see. Britain remains a source of unrivalled ingenuity and invention. But are we not putting too much of that invention into generating turnover and appearing to make money, year on year, without an eye to the deeper, longer consequences?

8

THE NEW CLASS SYSTEM – WHY DOES IT MAKE US SO MISERABLE?

I was part of that strange race of people aptly described as spending their lives doing things they detest, to make money they don't want, to buy things they don't need, to impress people they don't like.

Emile Henry Gauvreau
(1891–1956)

That man is the richest whose treasures are the cheapest.

Henry David Thoreau
(1817–1862)

Money is a good servant, but a bad master.

Aristodemus (4th century BC)

Children say money can't buy happiness.

Headline in the *Independent*,
March 2000

47% of workers in the UK feel that work rules their life, 52% of people in the UK feel that their jobs are going to get more stressful, 22% of all UK workers take sick leave due to stress.

Key findings in a study of public experience of stress at work,
The Samaritans/nfpSynergy, December 2007

Start with the ruling class. Ask a silly question. When did you last see a driver of a Mercedes smile at the wheel? Two blokes in a van, often cheerful; giggling lasses in a Ford Fiesta; we have all met them. But smiling Merc drivers? Never.

Why? In brief, while the Management are in control, they live in fear that they will lose control. And the more they seek to control through subterfuge or subtle coercion rather than respect or consensus the harder it gets. Anyone who has skippered a sports team of individuals when those individuals do not necessarily respect that skipper will know the feeling. There are established deductions as to how good teams work, a natural interaction of drive, perception, reflection, expertise, etc. That is to some extent skewed when politics, process or finance overrides all else. Such people find it hard to trust, they become insecure and defensive, work harder and delegate less. It is not an easy lifestyle.

These people are also under intense pressure to perform. It is now widespread practice for pay packages to include a large performance-related element or bonus. Again, this starts top-down, with many senior people being incentivised with bonuses larger than the sums earned all year by others. Now, imagine a manager who is highly strung and highly motivated, being incentivised to cut cost. Look at the pressure. Success, in the narrow sense, is often achieved; the target is met. But is it any wonder that many push the boundaries, slip into bullying, cut corners, fiddle results or targets, or turn a blind eye to sharp practice? And the sufferers are found at every level, though the ruling class have got the best of it. The rest are in much less control of their destiny.

THE SUPPORT TEAM

Those who work in Management Support do not have a particularly fulfilling time either. Most know that much of their output is in itself of limited value. They labour on, knowing that they could probably contribute more. Their frustration is illustrated by the established triangle in procurement: the choice between good service, quick service and cheap service. Management Support can only measure speed and price, so – guess what? – the quality goes down. Wealth Control see speed and price. Unfortunately it is usually the rest of the population who see the poor quality. Personal service has not gone out of fashion; it's just been more or less obliterated by Wealth Control as having little financial value.

WEALTH GENERATION – THE NEW WORKING CLASS

And then there is the real working class. As the exhausted construction gangerman once summed it up: 'They think we run on ****ing diesel.' Given that Management Support only look at speed and price that is probably quite near the truth. The result of all this is that society puts itself under pressure to go faster, push harder, just to survive.

Remember, also, Norman Tebbit trying to justify differentials between high and low earners through the concept of 'trickle down'. What an overwhelming level of disdain is achieved in those two words! Trickle? A sort of minor spillage, of limited volume, probably somewhat unintentional and generally to be regretted. Down? A brilliantly unconscious comment on the perceived power of money. It seems strange now, but he was trying to sell the benefits of government policy, as felt by the working class.

DEPENDANTS

It is almost a surprise that Dependants appear in these lists. They are not really considered. It is almost as if they are Dependants, full-time, with nothing else to do but... depend. And, children apart, with so many of the safety nets having been removed, they actually have to actively *work* at being dependant. Fill in forms, apply for jobs, trundle into distant post offices, and fight reduced allowances. We are getting used to seeing the 'haves' get richer; Dependents are the 'have-nots' who are quietly suffering the squeeze.

THE SQUEEZE ON SERVICE

And what happened to the idea of service to others? WRVS, meals on wheels, public service at work? One of the human behaviours that gives the most satisfaction – service – is now largely seen only as a means to an end. Good service these days means one of two things. Either it is something which needs to be exploited to generate profit, or it is a burden which a profit-making organisation cannot afford.

For an example of the first there is the story of one of the great reliable brands of washing-up liquid, whose makers hired consultants with a view to increasing profits. A simple idea emerged – to put a bigger nozzle on the bottle. More waste equals greater turnover and profit. And the product no longer provides quite the same level of outstanding service to householders. The flip side of service is seen at a leading high-street electrical retailers. They generally provide a pushy, cynical service and are massively profitable. So, when competition enthusiasts talk about choice, the choice is nasty and cheap on the high street or two sets of cheap and nasty in the retail park.

There are mechanisms that explain the cost of service. Resources equals cost. So, when you phone a business that you have paid to serve you, after you have paid up, what happens? They rarely phone back, you have to push the issue, and persist. In effect, you often have to organise their people. You are being required to organise them to provide the service for which you have already paid. It is brilliant because it saves them so much money and costs you time, which they do not have to pay for.

There is another effect; that businesses which do try to provide service cannot compete on costs with the others. Result – more complaints, more bolshy customers, more stress, more cheap and nasty and bye-bye user-friendly washing-up liquid.

A QUESTION FOR ALL OF US – WHO MAKES THE RUSH?

Start by asking yourself when you last went out for an evening. It may well have been a rush to get out; it may have produced a feeling of guilt at more pressing tasks undone; you may well have been too tired to really enjoy it. These are the basic symptoms of overwork. Under pressure, the first things that go are not the necessities but the nicer things of life; escapism, culture, theatres, school sport and celebrations of heritage. It has not been the best of twenty years for these. Of course, what is worse is that it does not make profits, so it does not appear to be of value to the management. And into the breach has stepped the internet; 60 million souls interacting not with each other, but a soulless animated rectangle that is infested by advertising.

THE ROLE OF ADVERTS

Another cultural shift has been the increasingly difficult task of avoiding advertising. Try it. BBC *Comic Relief*, a monstrous midway namecheck on receipt of a big cheque from Sainsbury's; movies with subliminal advertising; multinationals targeting eight-year-olds and hitting the target. And the influence of the Wealth Control lot is such that adverts persuade most people to respect their values. Even TV soaps are under pressure to find bigger stories, more episodes, in order to bring in the measurable result of more revenue. Adverts leave us to believe that unless we show our wealth we are not quite good enough. Just remember the advert that asked 'Inadequate car?' Focus owners want a Mondeo; a Mondeo man must aspire to a Volvo estate; Mitsubishi Shogun… Sherman Tank. Consumerism is being fuelled by envy, – an organised envy, deliberately sent out under the command of Wealth Control.

Remember, if distributed fairly, there is enough food, heat, light and shelter for everyone. Is it enough? Anyone can fall victim to a bit of despond, jealousy, sloth etc., but for an almighty downer, nothing beats a well-targeted advert.

The various tracks identified above run towards one conclusion: that style matters more than substance. There are plenty of lawyers who have no need for flash cars, but their peers start to question their credibility if they do not run one. Remember the cult for power dressing. 'Greed is good,' said Gordon Gekko in *Wall Street*, and the twenty-first-century version is probably not joking any more. Do we really have to believe that a life is less valid for not having brought great wealth? The result is an unhealthy emphasis on appearances and the measurable aspects of life. In many organisations there is more credit given to those who excel in project manipulation rather than project management. Most organisations include several highly paid people whose main contribution to the cause is to present in style and tick boxes. They are dependent, of course, on the efforts of others who, rather naïvely some might say, just do the job and make no fuss about it. These organisations are merely smaller Mammonocracies, built on the same principles as the main model.

9

THE NEW CLASS SYSTEM – WHY IT PUTS SOCIETY UNDER PRESSURE

At one fire station in Brighton, only three of the thirty firefighters can afford to live in the city they protect.

Julie Birchill in the Guardian, 2002

A desperate young mother who might not pay for a necessity in a supermarket or store can be branded a thief. A well-heeled young man accused of defrauding a leading bank of billions of euros is called a rogue trader.

Keith Nolan, letter to The Times, February 2008

A market-driven economy will always produce homelessness. We have places – old pit villages for instance – where all the work has gone, houses are boarded up and people are moving to work in other parts of the country where there is no housing for them. It doesn't make sense.

Ken Loach, director of Cathy Come Home (1966),
reported in the Guardian, February 2008

Many farmers and growers are in contracts which supermarkets never put in writing and the terms of which can change overnight. They are often asked to pay supermarkets for the privilege of trading. We are asking the question – how can you run a business in such a climate of fear?

Richard MacDonald,
Director-General of the National Farmers' Union, April 2008.

P eace, prosperity, and the management says everything is under control. But how often do you see a smile, on a train, in a car, or on the street corner? Crowds of people carrying their troubles on a worried face. Ask yourself why.

A DISTORTED HUMAN GEOGRAPHY

It is easiest to start with the physical. Some areas are seemingly packed solid, from London to the south coast; others are practically deserted, such as East Yorkshire. We have seen how the money follows the control, the control follows the money and so on. So, the financial centre, London, is unbelievably crowded and much of the countryside deserted. Does London provide food, manufacturing capacity? No, it provides services and uses more people than ever to do it. And one of George Osborne's first responses? Regional Pay.

The effects mean that the centre is so much more profitable than the outside; the people from the centre can buy up large portions of the shires. Second homes, little places for the weekends. To the London rich, some parts of the country have become little more than gardens for enjoyment at the weekend. Ask yourself who owns much of the property in the Lake District or rural Gloucestershire; these days it's not often those who were born there. And what fun is there, for locals, in living in a ghost town for five days and then having the weekend agenda dominated by those who arrive on a Friday night? And on the other side of the coin, how many nurses can afford to buy a property in London? Has anyone ever measured the efficiency of our usage of our residential property stock, in the way, say, that hotel groups measure 'occupancy rates'. Who knows, we might not need so many new houses, after all.

A DISTORTED WORKFORCE

The same distinctions apply to the functional divisions of the work force. An example of this is farming. The group of people who could have profitably run a farm twenty years ago can now run one many times the size. Where have the profits gone? To the gang masters, and not the gangs; to the supermarkets and not the farmers. The beneficiaries of the profits are shareholders in the supermarkets, based more in the South East (or the tax havens). The big money, and its support, has left the countryside and moved towards the financial centre. It was said during the foot-and-mouth crisis that Britain's farming industry was worth less than the tourist industry. That twists the truth: surely, the value of the farming industry has not changed. It is merely that the value has been transferred to the retail sector, controlled by supermarket shareholders, etc. from those in the farming sector.

INFRASTRUCTURE – TAKING THE STRAIN

One great reflection on our current inefficiency can be found with a look at the roads. They're crowded with people criss-crossing each other, rushing to get to work. Relatively few are using public transport. There are patterns here as well; go back a stage. What is the cheapest way this year of getting an element of productive work done? Just for a short period, use cheap agency labour and set them up on a zero hours contract. Avoid commitment. Move on to the next project. And the cheapest way of getting there: use a car. What is the point in arranging to live near a bus route or station if there is no predicting where the next job may be? Especially if the train service is poor, and the bus slow because there is no conductor. No wonder the roads cannot cope. They have become a repository for all the problems generated by the lack of long-term planning, of transport and much else. Of course the loss of amenity is borne by everybody, but where are the savings being used? Hospitals, railways, schools? Not so much. QCs' fees, council Chief Execs who get more than the PM and government franchise chiefs on £1,000 a day, tax-efficient. Nice if you can get it.

THE SKEWING OF PRIORITIES

There are plenty of behaviours which skew priorities away from that of maximising public benefit, i.e. optimising service. Start with the NHS, where we have the hospital consultants who are encouraged to carry out private work for higher fees than the NHS can afford.

For another frustration look at infrastructure maintenance. Most councils' policy is now to prioritise road maintenance issues, not to address the most fundamental problems but to reduce the likelihood of lawsuits. Statistics dictate this policy. You try getting safety signs erected unless there has already been a fatality. It is a powerful example because the result is that roads are, as a result, maintained to the state that they are just, but only just, not falling apart. Of course the logic applies to schools, hospitals and the rest; significantly, it is not quite the way that money men – ruling class – maintain their Audis or lawyers their share portfolios. Consider how many operations are set back through one of the necessary participants being unavailable. How many research programmes are shelved due to lack of funds? It happens all the time. Do the courts find the same difficulty when a case has to be heard? Do injunctions or company accounts get put in the pending tray because there is no one there to process them? No, the resources are there, because the ruling class demands them.

ALL CRIMES ARE EQUAL?

There is another example of the skewed culture produced by Wealth Control. Why does white-collar crime seem to matter little, and petty theft matter more? Black, Maxwell and friends got a rather more ambivalent response to their activities – and stole a whole lot more – than the average petty thief. Why? One crime generates turnover for Wealth Control, but the other does not. When serial bankrupts, Maxwells, etc. go wrong, they do not get a second chance because of some Christian ideal: surely this is because they generate a lot of work for Wealth Control. As for a drugged-up robber, he really is of little use to the management and so he goes to jail. And Farepak losers... are just losers.

'Competition' – divide and rule in a new guise

To learn more, go back to that word 'competition'. The great emphasis on competition also encourages people to look at the individual ahead of the corporate. Many organisations now set up internal competitions such that departmental heads compete to provide the cheapest solutions or the most accurate out-turn cost estimates. In some large organisations the harshest fights are internal; the corporate body is hoping to profit by pitting individuals against each other. And, note, there is little reference to quality.

The other effect of competition is the erosion of teamwork. Indeed, we are all mercenaries now. Yet who would you ask for support first? Friend, colleague or a mercenary? Our system determines that we all have to work together; competition pushes us the other way. And a recently detected side effect is seen in a recent survey, which indicated that three quarters of schoolchildren cheat at school sport. Given the fact that, in school sport, the result hardly matters, it makes you wonder how much cheating goes on when the result *does* matter.

Is anything sacred from 'commercial pressures'?

Of course not all our national sporting and cultural occasions have suffered. But they have changed. Are they primarily cultural or commercial events? There has been a shift of emphasis. Remember the joy of 'Peoples' Sunday' at Wimbledon a few years ago; off the cuff, spontaneous and not a single corporate guest was there, just genuine tennis people. The Royal Opera House, in bed with Travelex and Deloitte. Roy Keane knew the distinction when he complained about the 'prawn sandwich brigade' who added no atmosphere and crowded out the enthusiastic supporter. The romance of the FA Cup? Not so likely when Chelsea Village Mercenaries take on Arsenelle, Deuxième XI. The London Olympics, at venues they could have filled twice over and, until the public raised a fuss, there were rows of empty seats, thanks presumably to those who hadn't the enthusiasm to go with their privileges. The list goes on but the themes are the same – merit, culture, soul and individualism playing second fiddle to money and control.

STRESS AND CULTURE

In the end we go back to one of the first observations about current GB plc: stress and the role of culture. Culture is surely the issue that sets humans apart from all other forms of life. And yet Wealth Control would have us believe that it has little value. Actually, the rest of us instinctively know better; it is just that Wealth Control have made it unfashionable to articulate it. Culture is our means of escaping, briefly, from stress and worry. Mrs Thatcher can be said to have put her finger on the pulse of British culture. Unfortunately, she seemed to want to leave it there until the pulse stopped. She saw the cost and could not appreciate the benefit.

Besides, no one has the time any more. We are so busy fulfilling the roles allocated to us by the Wealth Control project that we have no time for the private projects that are our lives.

10

GB – Team or plc?

You show me a capitalist, and I will show you a blood-sucker.

Malcolm X
(1925–1965)

£3 million – the average final salary pension for FTSE 100 company CEO, about 40 times the average for other employees.

Statistics presented by Brendan Barber,
TUC general secretary, in New Year Message, 2007

The British Medical Association (the doctors' union) is threatening mass resignations from the health service if they are forced to open in the evening. This is what happens when you commercialise the NHS. Doctors become businessmen, not public servants. This has already happened in dentistry. You can't get an NHS dentist in some areas because they can earn so much more by going private.

Paul Routledge, *Daily Mirror*, February 2008

This is where it gets personal. This is where we look at how the average member of society is affected by the various trends already explained. What emerges is how the current system affects, generally helpfully, those within Wealth Control, and how the opposite applies to the rest. This is about where the rewards go and where they should go, in relation to the common good. Let us start with one of President Kennedy's more resonant phrases. 'Ask not what your country can do for you but what you can do for your country.'

VALUE JUDGMENTS

We can start by looking at a role, job or title and making judgement as to the value of it in society and the wider world. Ignore notions of respect. Be basic and unemotional. Ask yourself, what is the use of it? Yes, we can see that farm labourers help to put food on our tables. The conditions are crude and the pay is awful. Look at nurses: you will gladly seek their help when racked with pain but many feel they are taken for granted. Car mechanics: essential to most of us, but it is a messy business and the pay is poor.

Now move to the Wealth Control personnel. What does a lawyer have to show? An argument won. So what? Does it put food on the table? Does it bring in foreign currency? Does it assist society to be at ease with itself? Rarely, but the pay is good. Even better, a tax accountant, hired to ensure a company is tax efficient. Big salaries here. And, get this: this person is handsomely rewarded for looking at ways of *avoiding* contributing to the common good. How perverse is that? Fund managers who look for rising shares; the people who do well when a company announces rationalisations i.e. job cuts; they are usually rewarded best when others, whom they influence, act *against* the common man. So, go back to President Kennedy's phrase. The clear winners in the review above are those who have worked out what the country can do for them, while the rest are the losers.

There is also an apartheid that applies to the care taken over types of work. Take the contrast between safety of industrial operations and security of finance. Virtually anyone can get work in construction and farming, where safety standards are appalling. The losers are labourers and steel erectors, and they pay with their lives. And the beneficiaries are large corporations, who get cheap buildings and cheap food. Here's the contrast: have you ever heard of casual labour from Eastern Europe being used to check accounts or practise at law? An accountant's mistake never physically hurt anyone. So the nation pays well over the odds for finance and legal services, while those groups pay very little to others.

TEAMWORK AND GB PLC

Of course, by putting Wealth Generators in a competitive market, an adversarial atmosphere pervades. And it is then natural of the participants to take the hardest stances, the most obstinate positions. Great for teamwork. So when Government asks us, as it does occasionally, to 'all pull together in these difficult times', it follows that a good few – and MPs are a good example here – will say 'We'll get out of this what we can.' And others will say 'We'll do nothing more than we have to.'

It was Vince Cable who, in early 2008, warned that the government's attitude towards Northern Rock was akin to privatising the profits and nationalising the debt. The point was well made in relation to Northern Rock. But it extends far wider. Consider the principles. Do they not apply to PFI, immensely profitable for operators but crippling many hospital trusts? Remember Metronet, which was titled a Public Private Partnership? When it folded the private participants ended with losses of tens of millions, a fraction compared to the £1.7 billion liability inherited by the taxpaying public. Go back to foreign labour in hotels; hotel chains rack up profits while Local Authorities incur the liabilities. Actually, it is a recurring observation throughout this book.

Yes, GB plc has a strong and unified management culture. But it only reflects the values of a smallish element of the population. Just refer back to the values by which the City operates. When a firm announces redundancies the share price goes up. Good news! 7,000 sacked! Smiles in London, more money for shareholders and no jobs in the factories. Of course, fewer shareholders are found in Humberside, the Welsh valleys or the Potteries. The worry is that the winners have been so successful that the country has started to resemble a game of Monopoly where one or two players have all the property and the rest are gradually going bust. What we are moving towards, to coin a phrase, is Endgame Capitalism.

MONEY EQUALS POWER

There appears to be a logical conclusion here, that power is measured now more by pounds than votes. That sounds rather extreme. But are people really interested in general elections any more? Less than they were. Why? Is it not because they only marginally affect the management of the country? Nearly thirty years ago, Wealth Control was put to work as a tool of democratic government. Is it not now the case that Government has become merely a tool of the forces of Wealth Control? Wealth Control has become so strong that the elected management is to a great extent secondary. There are those who say that GB plc is a meritocracy. No, it is a Mammonocracy.

NO MONEY, NO INFLUENCE?

When you are next stuck in a traffic jam, get poor service from a once sound organisation, or hear of a viable business going under, do not shrug. Do not casually say to yourself, 'Bad luck' or 'It's one of those things.' Instead, remember this: most things that go on in our society have been planned; most things that go on in any organisation occur as the management plan it. When the organisation lets people down, it usually does so by design. So, when there are potholes or overcrowded trains, it is not because the maintenance gang are no good or the rail staff are incompetent, but because the investment is not there. And those on the front line see the frustrations and get the complaints, but there are then several degrees of separation from the chaos to its authors. The guys on the platform report to their supervisors, who report to managers, who are probably really members of the 3 B's. And they in turn report back to more senior management, whose roles and targets are determined at a separate level again, in Government, And the poor baffled traveller on platform 10 has as much connection to a Mongolian herdsman as he has to the decision maker with whom he would really like to take up his complaint. As the book asked, why is everything shit? The usual answer: because somebody, over whom the rest of us have very little influence, cut the budget, so that's all you're likely to get.

11

AND HOW IS GB plc DOING THESE DAYS?

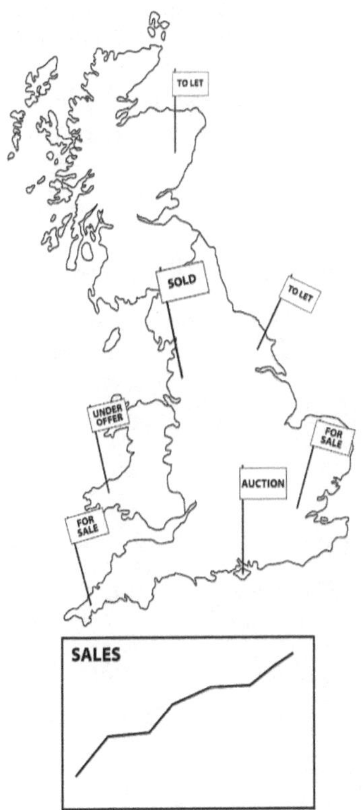

Economic inequality in the UK stands at historically high levels and there is emerging evidence that a high level of inequality may cause socio-economic problems.

From the Joseph Rowntree Foundation website.
Reproduced by permission of the Joseph Rowntree Foundation.

Complacency and silence could destroy liberty and democracy as effectively as tanks and guns.

Unnamed Czechoslovakian dissident,
1977, recorded by John Pilger

The highest use of capital is not to make more money but to make money do more for the betterment of life.

Henry Ford
(1863–1947)

Are the lights going out on British Science?

Headline of article on government cutbacks,
the *Daily Telegraph*, January 2008.

So, we did well to stay out of the Euro, share values are close to record highs and rating agencies still rate GB plc as a relatively low risk? GB plc is doing OK and is better equipped to deal with recession than most. Isn't that OK then? Well, perhaps not. Let us, in the interests of fairness of course, apply the measures used by Wealth Control within GB plc to measure how GB plc is doing in the rest of the world.

IS GB PLC TURNING A PROFIT?

Let's start with the big issue: profits. How do we measure this? It is the balance of money coming into the business against money going out. The Balance of Payments. Remember that? It is crudely a measure of whether the country makes a profit in its trade with the rest of the world. Guess what, it is running at an annual loss over 3% of our Gross Domestic Product. In other words, the company/country makes a 3% loss on annual turnover. Is this sustainable? Well, would you invest in the shares of a company that makes a loss, and where there is no sign of improvement? Would you invest in a property trader who does one hundred deals a year but breaks even by selling three properties more than she buys, or, for that matter, a farm that sells a field or two each year? It cannot go on. Is GB plc a loss-making company? Well, put it this way: the behaviour of loss-making companies gives a classic picture of the problems facing GB plc today.

THE LOSS-MAKERS IN HISTORY

Now have a look at what happens to a company that is running at a loss. The first effect is that the rates at which it can borrow money go up. Banks charge higher rates for higher risk. If the company returns to profitability the problem goes away; if not, the choices get rather harder. If all other things remain equal and the losses continue, the interest rate goes up as the cumulative risk goes up. Alternatively, the lender finds another way, by swapping assets for the debt. There is only one alternative: the lender pulls the plug. Britain's banking is, in effect, provided by the rest of the world, and like all competent banks, the rest of the world is quietly raking in interest from us and acquiring our assets.

THE SUBSIDIARIES OF GB PLC

Of course, Wealth Control have not sought to share the perception noted above. The bigger picture has to be assembled from the pieces of British industry. Try thinking of British firms as minor subsidiaries of GB plc. For the first result, take a 25-year review of an apparently successful privatisation, BT. By any reckoning, it should be a major player, but it cannot compete at world level because of historic debts. It can provide the technology, the management, the size, but cannot compete as strongly as it wants because of debt. It has had to downsize in order to operate within its means. And for every BT there are hundreds of smaller firms with the same problem.

For the second model, look at the likes of AstraZeneca, British Steel, Jaguar or many of the privatised utilities. Here, instead of downsizing, part or all of the firm has been sold out of GB. The show goes on, but the big decisions are partly made abroad, and these usually get taken to suit other interests than those of people in GB plc. Of all the outcomes this is the most sinister for GB plc's future. The process is the exact reversal of the policy that made GB plc great: colonisation. We are inviting others to take over and control our economy. Go back to the Raj and ask whether GB or India got the better deal. Now look and ask whether GB plc or Germany is getting the better deal out of the Mini brand being part of BMW. Let's not forget that when Motorola started to struggle to sell mobile phones, the plant in Scotland closed, with 3,000 jobs gone. On the same day, did Motorola HQ in America put as many thousand onto the dole queue?

And there is a third group: they are the busts. Laker, Barings, BCCI, Woolworths. There is little explanation needed here. Just look into the hole and gawp at the size of it. And the rest of the world moves in to fill the hole. To their advantage. Cor! Isn't that all a bit gloomy? Well, try this for a challenge: name a world class company (and you are not allowed to say the much hated Tesco) which remains wholly or even largely owned within GB plc?

GLOBAL COMPANIES

The wider picture, the completed jigsaw, has to be viewed in conjunction with another factor: global companies. The very biggest companies are no longer of a single nationality, or even just two or three. Ford UK is one of dozens of offshoots of Ford worldwide, a company that invests in products to be sold around the globe. But what matters is influence at the top tables; which is why the dilution of GB control of GB industry matters so much. What is this dilution, other than foreign takeover by agreement? Inward investment is a sector of GB plc which has been hailed as a great success. Semiconductors in South Wales, Nissan and Toyota and the rest. Yes, we get jobs, but who takes away the big profits or, if things go wrong, decides to pull the plug? The point is that the control has gone, surrendered abroad. Long-term control surrendered for short-term gain. History gives us an uncomfortable precedent: King Ethelred 'the Unready', who paid the Danes to go away.

THE WAY THE MONEY GOES ROUND

The debate about GB plc cannot avoid another issue: the value of our currency. When Harold Wilson, in the 1960s, said that a devaluation would not affect the value of 'the pound in your pocket' he was avoiding the global truth. The worth of goods produced in GB plc is measured not in pounds but in dollars, euros, yen and the rest. GB incomes are measured in the cost of foreign goods and holidays, as well as food and the staples of home life.

But, the strength of an economy is not solely measured by the strength of its currency. The experience of 2008 told us that our habit of trading at a 3% loss makes us highly vulnerable. Yes, we did well to stay out of the Euro and it has given us the option to devalue. But, despite devaluation we are still trading at a loss, it is affecting our credit rating; 'confidence' in the ability to repay can be fragile. We should remember how it could all get a lot worse quickly.

The problem is best explained by the solution. It is the combination that the money men absolutely hate. Lower interest rates, devaluation, mild inflation. Gadzooks! Yes, you read it right. Devaluation and inflation. Now, keep reading. The inflation will tend to make us spend less and, as devaluation occurs, we will import less; for example, we can afford fewer foreign holidays and properties abroad. Our own goods will gradually become, globally, cheaper, so we should export more. That way, we will move towards a trade equilibrium with the rest of the world, or, in other words, paying our way. And lower interest rates, together with the accompanying devaluation is the only way in which new trade, with a reduced burden from interest charges, previous commitments, etc., will produce new wealth. The Balance of Payments matters; we are living beyond our means, and an unsustainably high exchange rate should be seen primarily as a method for doing so. We are back to where we were before Black Wednesday, in 1992. The laws of economics dictate that it has to change.

WHO BENEFITS NOW?

There is one other interesting observation regarding these outcomes: the way in which they affect the Wealth Control membership and the different way they affect everyone else. Who benefits from high interest rates? Bankers, the rich, those with money to lend. You see, it suits those in Wealth Control for the nation to be cash rich; they are in a position to milk it. Here we see again another recurring pattern: the management appear to be selling the nation's longer-term future in order to increase turnover, to generate the cash from which they secure their futures. Private profit and nationalised liabilities. Remember that GB plc, in 2007, a boom year, made a loss of around £40 billion, that's about £600 per person, over the year.

A really frightening comparison is with the recent example of a major US corporation whose management indulged in ever more intricate and daring fiddles to show that the company was making more profits and had an increasing worth of assets. Their accounts were audited by the leaders in their field. As this occurred, the company paid its managers higher and higher salaries. It then went spectacularly bust. Could GB plc turn into a slow-burning Enron? Let's hope not.

12

AND THE FUTURE?

The property market has created a generation gap between those in housing wealth and those who have little or no chance of accessing those assets. We cannot allow the next generation to continue to be locked out of the housing market or the economy will feel the full force in the future.

Shelter press release, More than 8 out of 10 young people
'worried about housing', 6 November 2007

It's perhaps a sad indictment on the present age that we accept the need to help parents to play their part – to rediscover what being a parent means.

John Dunford, general secretary of the Association
of School and College Leaders, March 2008

With weak legal and institutional structures and the profit motive of accountancy firms, audit failures are institutionalised too. But accountants make money at every stage. More Enrons are inevitable, though the scale might differ. Greater reforms are needed as major firms have close links with government departments, senior civil servants and political parties.

Prem Sikka, Professor of Accounting,
University of Essex, February 2002

Employers are increasingly worried about the long-term decline in numbers studying A-level physics, chemistry and maths, and the knock-on effect on these subjects and engineering at university. They see, at first hand, the young people who leave school and university looking for a job, and compare them to what they need. Increasingly, they are looking overseas for graduates.

Richard Lambert,
CBI Director-General, August 2006

THE ECONOMY

This is where it all gets a little scary. OK, so there is a strong management culture in GB plc, but the awkward truth is that the current management has succeeded in exploiting the economy as much as it can, year on year, and the economy is now showing the strain. The bits that matter, long-term, are beginning to fall behind: infrastructure, education, research, new products, world-class British companies. The background: globalisation.

THE POSITION OF GB PLC

Let us be clear: we should see ourselves, as GB plc, in competition with the rest of the world. If the Chinese can make toys cheaper than we can, they will get the income; likewise, Indians taking a greater share of the IT business. People in the UK drive Japanese cars because they are safe to run and cheap to buy. The questions is, where is the role, in a worldwide sense, for an ageing population with comparatively primitive education, few new ideas and little development support? For an understandable model, just look within the UK at a company that can no longer compete. We know what happens: it goes bust, or sees a reduction in its influence, or merges.

A SKEWED LEGACY

Next, look at the next generation, who are trying to take on the company, the next board members of GB plc. What sort of grounding are they getting? Aren't they growing up in the belief that the real high-fliers are accountants and lawyers. So that is where all the talent will go. And the other side of this is that real work, the 'doing', 'making', 'helping' will be seen as second-rate. The message that the next generation will receive is to pursue

Wealth Control roles and not Wealth Generation. In simpler terms, this translates as 'Don't just do something, sit there!' So the brightest and best get to play number games, enact arguments and court popularity, leaving the rest, with less training and less ability, to attempt to compete abroad. When Manchester United play in the biggest games, they put out their strongest team; at present GB plc appear to send the reserves and keep the cream for the internal battles.

The lasting effects of Wealth Control on the next generation are much wider than simply economic. Has there ever been a more inward-looking generation than the present ruling class? Aren't the current management so busy working to keep up the present appearances that the next lot can be forgiven for thinking that no one is interested in them? Take a child's view: long periods at the childminder's, parents working away four nights a week, stress due to overwork and insecurity… toys, money and a well-equipped home, but little love and attention. And the results where there is little love, care and affection? No wonder that knife crime occurs and drugs become attractive. The urge to be destructive or rebellious is nurtured where love, care and affection come second to other things. Children's capacity for love, friendship and self-development has huge resilience but it is not limitless.

OUR ISLAND STATE

The other facet of Wealth Control is the insularity of the British model. Of course, this inward-looking habit is not entirely accidental. The management do not wish us to look outside. They have got us where they want us. As we have said, to an extent they are currently selling our future in order to secure theirs. The longer they can stay in that little cocoon the better for them; they would prefer to milk GB plc for a few more years before any takeover. So, Europe is painted as a threat and a source of bureaucracy, rather than as one that provides, in some cases, a better long-term business model. Yes, the Germans run a very successful economy based on manufacturing and technology, but our leaders would prefer to back the City of London.

There is another disturbing model: the railway industry. A couple of years after the creation of Railtrack, the shares were triple their issue value, the annual reports positive and the future apparently assured. OK, the word from the trackside and from the commuters was of crumbling facilities and meaningless targets. Now ask which was the truth, the word on the streets or the word of the management? You know the answer. Now, apply the same observations to GB plc. Which is right, street or management?

There is a final cruel trick to play on the eye when looking at GB plc's future. Take a map of Europe and turn it completely upside down. Now try and assess the significance of the small group of islands at the bottom right-hand corner. It looks about as significant as Greece, for example. Yes, a nation on the periphery of world events, with a fascinating history, curious climate, shambolic capital, crumbling transport system and a weak economy. If you want GB plc to remain viable, it's time for a new management before it's too late.

13

So What Do We Do About It?

He who knows how to be poor knows everything.

Jules Michelet
(1798–1874)

We must be the change we want to see in the world.

Mahatma Gandhi
(1868–1948)

I think people are getting genuinely fed up and saying 'I'm not going to sit around and wait, I'm going to vote with my feet.' There has been a definite rise in consumer action.

Alan Tattersall of uSwitch.com, a group active
in the energy market, February 2007

People who are arrogant about their wealth are about equal to our Laplanders, who measure a man by the number of his reindeer.

Fredrika Bremer
(1801–1865)

Evil flourishes when good men do nothing.

Edmund Burke
(1727–1797)

Who covets more is evermore a slave.

Robert Herrick
(1591–1674)

Money is only important when you don't have any.

Sting

Control your destiny, or someone else will.

Jack Welsh, 1994

As individuals

Firstly, if you believe the message here, tell others. Photocopy it, gossip, tell your friends. It is one of the great successes of the current management that no one has really spotted who they are and the short-sightedness of what they are doing. Well, you know now, and the more that others know about it the better. Remember, that until around 1988 estate agents just quietly carried on their business, unhindered by the watchful eye of regulators and other informed sceptics. Within a short period, their cover was blown, their credibility greatly reduced. Of course, most of them are still in business, but their excesses have since been curbed. It is more or less the same process that needs to be applied to Wealth Control, a much bigger and more powerful target. There is no need to destroy them, just to curb their pre-eminence. The acid test is during the introductions on a reality TV show; when an accountant gets booed, we can say that the tide has turned.

WE'RE NOT ALONE – PRESSURE GROUPS AND NETWORKS

There is now such a feeling of frustration at the way things are that dozens of pressure groups have sprouted. It is not just *Watchdog* any more. In fact, there is no industry or mega-corporation that does not have some sort of anti-corporation support network: Tescology (as a watchdog for Tesco), the Football Supporters' Association (the Premier League), moneysavingexpert.com (bank charges). On a lifestyle front, there is a group called We Are What We Do who have many suggestions, and a network together with a book entitled *Change the World for a Fiver*. Others are listed at the back of this book. And don't just vote with your feet, treat political parties as pressure groups. Use them and use your vote at election time.

WHAT WE CAN DO – DAY-TO-DAY AT THE WORKPLACE

Now for the day-to-day stuff of individual lives. Ask whether all of the hassle of work is worth it. What about giving up some money to make some time? Is it not true that most of those who have consciously 'downshifted' have no regrets at what started as a leap of faith? And don't some of the most miserable faces on the streets belong to those whose lives are rich in money and little else besides? For a start, try to avoid cramming the day with targets; it's a life, not a race.

IN THE HOME

What about ensuring that the television is not on simply 'by default'; there never will be enough hours in the day to catch all the programmes – and adverts – that might, just might, be worth watching. Try cooking slow food and eating it slowly: it's cheaper and healthier, too. And while we are on food, what about spending as much money but on less volume, more quality; look at the BOGOF as the product they cannot shift and, unless you're feeding seven, ignore it. Besides, overloading our stomachs is a waste of three highly valued commodities: food itself, healthy bodies and the NHS resource to treat the effects.

IN YOUR SPARE TIME

This sounds dumb, but try spending your spare time doing things that involve making your own entertainment and are, apart from the kit, free. Look at team sports, volunteering, the outdoors, music, gardens, DIY, making stuff, baking and cooking. Yes they take time and effort, but the rewards last longer; they generate new skills and new friendships and usually get you fitter. Contrast that with entertainment that you pay for, such as cinema, going to the match and shopping. Notice how, at each of these, there is copious advertising for the others, limited interaction with other people, and, at most stages of the process – booking fees, parking, refreshments, as well as the main event – a bit of cash goes missing.

PERSONAL FINANCES

Looking at finances, the response has to be to think what you *need* – not what others persuade you to want. Research indicates that the happiest people are those who neither hoard great amounts of money nor get into debt. The apparent recipe for happiness – or of avoiding unhappiness about money – is to spend what you have, but no more. What proves the point? This pattern of behaviour is never, ever advocated in adverts.

THE LESSONS OF MUTUALITY

Ask yourself why the banks hate mutuality. It means that mutual organisations can expose the sheer extent of the banks' profiteering. No wonder they were prepared to pay huge bribes to try and kill the concept of mutuality. As usual, the rule is that if the forces of Wealth Control think something is good, go the other way. Avoid that loan, use credit cards only when you can pay off the credit immediately. Remember, banks are there to provide a service to you; you pay for that service, so you should set the terms. Avoid their game, the one with higher stakes, in which you start with a big loan and they hold all the cards.

Of course, some of the lesson of mutuality applies to other issues. Consider investing in relationships, instead of shares; it is more rewarding and the value of people goes down far less frequently. Think of public transport as an extension of mutuality; a bus trundling down an empty road can outrun a Ferrari in a queue. If not we can look forward to crammed multi-lane motorways and the accelerated end of the oil. When it comes to shopping, use local shops; their income stays local rather than feeding a percentage of profit to Wealth Control types and shareholders. Yes, of course it is difficult to make these changes. Some are unfashionable, but if enough people do it, fashion will follow. Others simply involve more physical effort, which does no harm, or more preparation – OK, that's harder for families – which can be done in the time that previously went to TV and work.

How to enjoy adverts

There is also a way to enjoy adverts and not feel pressured. The secret is to be as cynical about the advertiser as they are about you. When you see a really slick advert the first thought is, 'Wow, they really tried hard there!' The second, empowering thought that should follow is, if such effort is needed, the product may not be that good. Why else does the advert exist? Because, of course, the product does not sell itself, and the supplier is desperate for you to buy. What a wonderful, empowering thought! Suddenly, you, the consumer are back in charge, where you should be, and it is the advertisers and the suppliers who are imploring you to buy their product. Just remember that crisp manufacturers spend far more on advertising than on making the product. Try selecting purchases by reference to personal recommendations, and making these to others. Who needs brand 'x'? Or, to appreciate the power of branding, take £200 worth of nearly new purchases to a car boot sale and see how hard it is to sell it for, say, £40; it is a graphic illustration of the capacity of advertising to get you to pay over the odds.

Challenge your information

When it comes to information, watch out again for the influence of Wealth Control. Remember who owns the newspapers, and adjust your interpretation to suit. If they back big business remember this: most are owned by big business. To misquote Mandy Rice-Davies, 'They would say that, wouldn't they?' Bear in mind that commercial television is largely paid for by adverts. It's an old saying, but when the piper plays, who calls the tune? When Government asks for consultants to prepare policy reports, do they take more notice of Greenpeace or PriceWaterhouseCoopers?

Whose time is it?

Time is money, they say. Ross McEwan, head of RBS, is paid a million pounds a year. He works a lot of hours, but he is paid every few days as much as a teacher or soldier in a year. And two and a half million are unemployed. It probably feels to them that they are worth nothing. Yes, Mammonocracy has created one of the unhappiest and one of the most unequal societies in the developed world. Nothing new? Historical figures from Greece, through Jesus, have referred to the rich and the poor. The 1662 wedding ceremony asks couples to take each other, for better or worse, for richer or poorer and so on. And ironically, today, there is a society that is much more unequal than GB plc; 'Communist' China.

Now, go back; time is money. Shall we set aside business speak and challenge that? This matters, because there are options as to what we do with our time. Firstly, we trade it. We call it work; we trade our time for money, influence, pension, favours, Argos vouchers, the means to pay the gas bill or go to the match, whatever. And when we do this, the more time we put in the more money we tend to get. But, secondly, there is other time; yes, be honest, there is time which we waste. Sitting in traffic, the internet, staring into space, TV and its adverts that plant covetous thoughts into empty minds. And, lastly, and usually least, there is time that we give. To each other. To creating, to caring, to societies, to volunteering. Isn't this when we come alive? Yes.

So, when we give time, what happens? One, we stop clock-watching, for this is enjoyment and fulfilment; nothing beats a labour of love. Second, giving starts a virtuous circle; recipient benefits too. Third, these are the memories that stay with us; those of us who write Christmas letters find that the 'giving times' supply most of the highlights. There are not many, who, on their deathbeds, have wished they had spent more time in business meetings, or watching repeats of Downton Abbey. And something else happens when we give time; we become equal. Massive. Ross McEwan may cost more when he trades his time at work, but, an hour of a father's love is... an hour of a father's love, whoever you are. When we give our time to others, talking, sharing a pastime, caring, listening, we become equal. Wonderful.

So, time is money? No; it's more important. None of us are here for long. Time is not, as has been said, the fourth dimension; it is the first. It belongs to us. And if 'giving' time is so good, memorable and worthwhile, and makes us all equal, let's put it first. We can still choose to trade or waste the rest. But we can start with time to giving … to each other, to the bigger things in life.

AND SO...

So, when your boss asks you to do a bit more, remember whose time it is. Make your own decisions, for yourself. Because we know what the management are for and the answer, too often has been, 'for themselves'. And if the management are following a loss-making, divisive and largely self-serving management model, then maybe we need to find a new management model – 'for ourselves'.

14

THE 2013 UPDATE

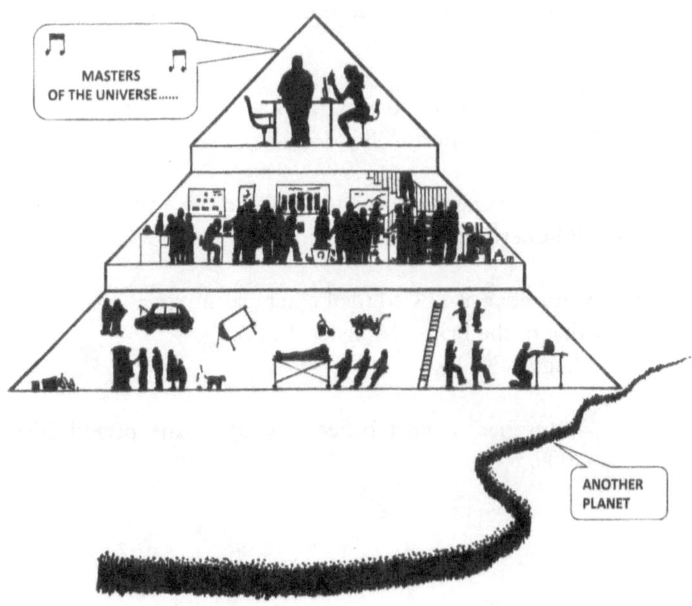

10   – ratio of house prices to average earnings in the Borough of Tower Hamlets, London, 2012.

15   – number of European countries with faster broadband provision than Great Britain, April 2012.

22   - percentage of 18 to 25 year olds in neither work nor higher education in UK, February 2012.

35   - Billions of pounds of UK tax 'avoided' by corporations, according to Public Accounts Committee, May 2012

56   - the number of council houses constructed in the last six years in London, 2006 to 2012.

75p   – the average hourly wage for cabin staff working for P+O cruises, March 2012.

114   - number of UK council chief executives at salaries above that of the Prime Minister, £142k, August 2011.

3932   - number of post offices closed in the period 2000 – 2009.

That was 2008; this is now

So, that was then, 2008; we have discussed what we can do as individuals. But, this update sets the analysis and messages in this book against the agenda of government and policy.

THE MAMMONOCRACY PYRAMID

First, let's go back to the Mammonocracy pyramid and review what it is that we were grumbling about. A poor economic outlook; an economy poorly positioned to compete. An economy where a great deal of the wealth is tied up in pension funds, shares and property; much more than is tied up in graduates, apprentices and industrial estates. An economy therefore that is set up to serve best those who already have their wealth, at the expense of those who are yet to have chance to make theirs. This is about a productive cohort who are having to carry too much of the baggage on behalf of others. So, those productive people who can carry our economy forward are staggering under the burden and it is no wonder that the tendency to dip is stronger than the tendency to recover. Double Dip, Triple Dip, or a "recovery" funded by debt? Unavoidable, unless the figures are fudged or economic policy is aligned to help those who are carrying the burden.

The preceding chapters have charted the weaknesses of the Mammonocracy pyramid. Let's now work down the pyramid and reflect how the understanding of the pyramid can inform policy.

WEALTH CONTROL – DO YOU ADD VALUE OR EXPLOIT IT?

Start with a few challenges for the current management. Does your work add, create or generate long term value? Good. Or does your work exploit value or avoid, evade or externalise cost? How are CEO's and board members rewarded? On the basis of share price or annual profits, metrics which reflect a horizon of between 1 to 5 or so years. Now, to explain why this may be mistaken, let's use a more glamorous example. A Grand Prix race. 195 miles or so. Does Lewis Hamilton get a monster incentive for leading after lap 12 out of 60? And using a quarter of the petrol for a fifth of the race? We recognise the symptoms; it is called 'turbo-capitalism' and it is fuelled by consumption of items like green fields, fossil fuels and, worst of all, people's efforts. And, as in a turbo, fuel gets burnt out, both real and metaphorical such as people. A few lucky souls get to go very fast for a short time and after that there is nothing.

So, when it comes to our managers and CEO's what do we need? Surely a more rounded view of the value of the ruling class has to emerge; the distinction is this.... their value should not be assessed on the money they can extract – in the short term that is evidently all too easy - but on the value they add to organisations and society – "measure me by what I give you". So, if a CEO transforms a company, maybe he is worth it; Dyson took his risk and is worth his reward. But we know that there are bankers and others who have taken little personal risk – rigging Libor rates, mis-selling PPI, doing well out of small businesses and 'muppets', etc – who have behaved with little more restraint than locusts. And this is not a personal gripe against those individuals; it is, more than anything else, just a crashing great waste of resource; one high-flier banker pays for 30 nurses or research assistants.

Since 2008 there has been a great deal of political discussion of executive pay, driven by public uproar. And the result? It does not say much for our democracy, but the gap, already wide, between the haves and have nots, has simply widened. The point is illustrated by our MPs' themselves. To many readers their pay of around £65k (plus those expenses) would appear highly desirable. And they think they deserve more. And to back their case, there are 100+ public jobs on offer at more than the PM is paid. Go back to the big picture; surely, the issue now about politicians is not that they are paid too little, but that a good few others, especially those to whom MP's make comparisons, are paid far too much.

Management support – what is the use of it all?

Remember the 3 B's? They are still out there. But, opinion is changing, and politics with it. Bureaucracy: aren't we gradually working out that more management is not better management? So, a public organisation such as a school will be inspected and assessed, on behalf of users, by 6 or 8 or more organisations, committees, statutory bodies or quangos; it must be very confusing - and expensive - for everybody. Why not have just one body, much as a supermarket has one Customer Services Department? Bullshit comes next: there are hundreds of examples but, come on, does the Home Office need 151 press officers, paid for by the public purse; is there so much that you guys need to explain? Last, beancounters; it is an obvious but unappreciated fact that beancounters do not save money. They just show the savings, so we don't need zillions of them do we? Do we need to check every line of every account, every month? And the point is this; too many of these people are simply absorbing resource that could go into supporting industry education and infrastructure at the front line.

Now that we can see why it matters, let's apply some distinctions to Management Support. Firstly, before everyone in our middle class rushes for the door; a good deal of it is essential and valuable, the structure on which civilised society is based. So, when IT lets us provide useful information and analysis, give credit; when beancounters ensure the accurate use of resources to meet genuine need, pay up, they're worth it; when bureaucracy protects people's rights, privacy and possessions that is a job well done. Again, what we are looking at here is the value that these people give, measured in relation to society as a whole.

Now to the stuff we do not want. Do you largely work 'for the boss', for management, or to ensure someone has a quiet life? Do you invent procedures that appear mainly to cover someone's back; do you major in media advice and presentation; do you spend your time defining 'accountability', often a codeword for blame; are you busy with reports, justifications, lawsuits, procedures or monthly accounts, for whom? Yes, it all helps the management and gives them a comfort blanket of assistance, but, crucially, will it be remembered or appreciated by your teenage niece? This is not about 'big government' or the opposite; this is the distinction between the stuff that largely only provides employment or serves managers or the building of a society fit for the 21st Century.

There is an associated matter of principle: should we not be putting empowerment ahead of procedures and multiple layers of supervision? Go back to the 3 B's. How many fraud or child abuse cases end up with everyone seeming able, in retrospect, to defend their conduct but then, also, no one seems to have felt empowered to intervene? Similarly, anyone who has run a publicly funded project will recognise the need for half a dozen or more signatures – business manager, project manager, procurement, for one funding decision. The effect, perversely, is to dilute clarity of responsibility; and it wastes yards of time.

There is a further, compelling reason for slimming down the 3 B's, demonstrated by a headline from 2009 that said "£100k fails to attract secondary school heads". Commenting on this, a former government adviser explained that ran "teachers are put off by the bureaucracy and the workload". So, not only is there direct waste, but there is a waste of productive talent going on here as well. What is going on? Is it not the case that the sheer volume of output of the 3 B's means that very few individuals have the brains, motivation and training to properly manage the massive administrative effort for which they take responsibility? Which pushes up those management salaries? Depressing? Yes, and then, when these people get overworked, what do they do? They hire more assistants! But there is a way out, and this is massively important, because, the spiral works both ways; if you cut the 3 B's you will, over time, reduce the workload involved in the management posts, increasing competition and making it easier to reduce those salaries. It's a tough target, but there are two potential wins with one hit.

WEALTH GENERATION – FOUNDATION OF THE ECONOMY

Now, let's do some more positive thinking; does your work add or generate value? Let's hope that your output is new ideas, research, development; nurturing, coaching, education; creating the next big thing; making, mending, building and preparing for sustainability? Brilliant, you're probably part of the solution. But, there are challenges for the new working class as well; are you trained, motivated and competitive? The working class, as we have defined them, need as much as any other class to be competitive; that means better, faster or cheaper than, say, Polish plumbers, Korean car workers or American pharmacologists.

So what can Government and the captains of industry do? They need to assist direct Wealth Generation and those things that assist it, using and generating skills, through work such as providing infrastructure, infrastructure, technology, energy and public works. We need to target expenditure to future Wealth Generation, repairing, doing and making, and by doing, preserving and adding to the skills that we have; for too long training budgets have been the first to be squeezed. We need to apply long-term valuing; and accept that some investment may not bring a return. Invest in ideas, willingly not grudgingly. Also, we have a short time to get ready for a sustainable future. And when technology moves on, as it does, there is no point in union leaders trying to preserve 400 'old' jobs; better to retrain for 250 new ones than watch all 400 float gently down the river. In brutal terms, a competitive world means that there will, increasingly, be only two types of members of the newly defined working class; those who offer a world-class combination of flexibility, skill and price and those who don't. Those who don't are at risk of being, in the wider sense, redundant.

DEPENDANTS – OUTSIDE THE PYRAMID

And finally, we look at the work needed to care for dependants. We think of serving and caring for others, unpaid caring; lots of basic stuff, the sort of work that makes the world goes round. We should start with the next generation but this is so big it needs a chapter of its own, Chapter 15.

At the other end of the scale, what is coming into view is the Care Crunch. We know there will be more aged dependants, mostly retired; we can also see lower real incomes and tax receipts, and it could set generation against generation. The same generational issue lies behind the poster 'hands off my pension'. Be clear, this is not the same as 'fair pensions for all'. Take the view from the next generation. Their retirement age is rising so fast as to be disappearing from sight. And then, at the same time, they are being asked to make their sacrifice in order to fund pensions for those in the late 50's who have paid in for 35 years, minus the odd holiday, and expect to claim a full pension from here on in, and have a life expectancy of a further 25 years. Sorry, but that does not look like 'fair pensions for all' and it does not look sustainable either.

TAXES

And this is where, like it or not, we have to talk about taxes. For a start they have to be fair and to be rigorously collected. Only that way will they be seen to be fair. So, if individuals want the benefit of the 'safety nets' of being in the UK, such as the NHS, for goodness sake make sure they pay, and are seen to pay UK taxes. So, if the likes of Starbucks, Dixons, Boots the Chemist, Walkers Crisps and Amazon want to trade as if they belong on the UK high street, can we not stop them declaring profit elsewhere to avoid UK tax? If nothing else, let's see their tax accounts; is this not an issue of public interest?

FUNDING ELECTIONS

The preceding chapters have said a lot about governments compromised and hobbled by ties to vested interests? So, surely, note to all three main parties: what is required is more fundamental than a mere change in Government. There needs to be a conscious separation of government from other influences, so that a Government's determination, as it is tested, is deflected as little as possible by ties to interest groups. That means elections funded by tax payers, not dodgy donors, PM's dinner guests or unions. And yes, as of 2010, all 3 parties saw the need, and in 2012, between them, they comprehensively fluffed it up. The fact is that tens of millions of pounds should do it, less than the tax some PLC's avoid in a month. And the point is that ordinary voters need to feel that they, not members of the Wealth Control club, have the main influence. To illustrate the weakness of our democracy our government is the main shareholder in two banks but they still seem unable - or is it unwilling? - to use their influence to radically change the behaviour of those who caused such problems in the first place.

'MANAGED DECLINE?'

An interesting concept was disclosed under the 30 year rule in relation to Mrs Thatcher and Liverpool in the Eighties. There was serious discussion of a policy of….. 'Managed Decline'. This has a grim resonance now. Government no longer makes any reference to the term 'regional policy', there is just a quiet progression to protecting the City above other things. Are we not seeing the start of a policy - unwritten - of Managed Decline for much of the country, mostly in order to protect interests in the City of London?

A year or two ago an example arose that demonstrated the narrow vision of Wealth Control, its effects and has an echo of Managed Decline. The example concerns the costs and benefits of rationalising Post Offices. We could start by being provocative; the cheapest option for a Post Office service would be just to have one really big one in London. But it is instructive to run through the pros and cons of closing a Post Office for each sector of our pyramid. First, our managers see lower visible costs; reducing a pension liability; a curbing of union power and a way of quietly building up business for allies, such as banks. And, as we now know, an easing of the path to private ownership Then to the new middle class: not much effect, a bit less admin, maybe. Then to the Wealth Generators: fewer Post Offices means a bit more travelling, more cost to use, and the service is less useful. Not good. And Dependants, the most vulnerable are the worst affected: less Post Offices means more dependency, more travelling, more cost to use. It is not as obvious as 'bedroom tax' or tuition fees but just as divisive.

THE BIG SOCIETY?

The post office example is also not all about money; there is another factor in the debate. This is about, to coin a phrase, 'soft infrastructure'. The Post Office is more than just a business, it is a vital part of that system of connections, services, shops, clubs, groups, societies and friendships that supports what we call a 'community'. And, of course, we see their value most when they are gone.

It may well be that David Cameron's Big Society is an attempt to describe soft infrastructure. Well done Dave, you have made a good point there. But you have completely missed the point that really matters. Yes, the Big Society, or soft infrastructure matters hugely. Its breadth, depth and history is one of the things that others admire about the UK. The message for you, Mr Cameron, is not, as you seem to, to see it as something to be exploited, to save money; it is something to be supported, to be celebrated and is one of the most valuable things we can pass on to the next generation.

So, before someone implements a cost cutting proposal, look at the big picture: is it merely externalisation of the cost - Cost Cutting, Transfer, Avoidance, Evasion and the rest - or is it a real saving to society at large? We need a government smart enough to spot the difference and brave enough to act on it. We need a Government to set an example of applying cost-benefit analysis holistically and for the longer term.

THE LONG HOURS CULTURE

And here is another issue, the long hours culture; who wins? This matters in several ways, for this is about wealth distribution too. When challenged in the press, the Chief Exec of our local council explained her £170k salary in terms of her doing 3 and a half jobs. Heroic, so heroic she then went on the sick for two months. But, surely, much more important, is this not just plain greedy? Put it another way, if one person does 75 hours a week and another is unemployed; what good does that do for the friends and family of either? Or for the graduate who cannot get a start. So, rather than painting the Working Time Directive as a European bureaucratic interference we should see it as a tool for a necessary redistribution of wealth. And if the work is more evenly shared, both the under-employed and the over – worked should both benefit. Yes, it's not that easy, but it is a powerful thought.

WHERE NEXT?

So, what is the point of all the distinctions in the paragraphs above?

Go back to the very start of this book. Wealth Generation and Wealth Control. At the moment the agenda is being set by Wealth Control, with the occasional concession to Wealth Generation. Think of Tuition fees, the 50p tax decision, the cuts. And it is not working? No, because, as explained above, it cannot work. Looking forward, policy needs to concentrate on putting life into dull old industrial estates, export markets, research and development, to favour Wealth Generation with the occasional concession to Wealth Control. And the longer we leave it we will be less able to pay our way in global markets. Yes, at present, we are making a 5% loss on turnover, our gross debt is now over 70% of annual turnover and is rising. Yes, we are living beyond our real means and, yes, our position is getting worse.

So, where next? Change is essential, the time for denial is over; the need for action becomes more immediate by the week.

15

And Now ... What About the Next Generation?

A CONVERSATION FOR OUR TIMES

A train waits, outside an English town. It waits for over an hour, just outside the station, this reported to be due to the suicide of a 'smartly dressed man'. In the train there is enough time for people, even the British, to get an urge to talk. 'There but for the Grace of God go I' offers a voice and it breaks the silence. At a set of 4 seats a banker is talking to the owner of a failed joinery business. They reflect that they have time for a bit of political and financial sparring as neither needed to hurry; the banker has been 'between jobs' for nine months and the other had only a night shift to look forward to, stacking shelves. They swap stories of bad decisions, failings and warnings they ignored. The banker finds himself saying 'it seemed a good idea at the time' a lot, to justify himself and the joiner merely refers to a succession of 'cunning plans' and all too readily refers to himself as a fool. They have been talking for some time when an older gentleman fills a pause in the discussion with a question:

'When a banker lends to a fool, who is the fool?'

More soul-searching, self – blame and banter results but the three surprise themselves with the unanimity of their conclusion, that the banker, the one with the knowledge, the understanding of risk, the charts, the big salary, is, fundamentally, the fool. The banker considers this briefly, but has largely stopped caring about the reputation of banks and instead, issues a question to the joiner:

'Ok, so what's your outlook, then?'

The joiner runs through some details of some of the debts that he knows are owed; he reckons he'll pay his debts in the end, but too far into the distance to say when. In the meantime he just takes whatever shifts come his way, weekends, the lot, and expects to do this…more or less… for ever. This puts a rueful smile on the older man's face. 'Sounds close to slavery to me', he mutters. No one argues. After another pause the banker speaks again, to the older man.

'I suppose you are comfortably retired?'

And, yes, the older man confirms that he is retired, but keeps himself busy with renovating a house in Wales and taking care of what he modestly describes as a few financial interests. The joiner perks up at the mention of the renovation, and the older man explains how Patryk from Poznan lives close by in a caravan and was helping him with brickwork, labouring, joinery, the lot; the locals just could not compete on price, or sheer energy and enthusiasm. The banker asks him, out of interest, where he invests these days; the older man remains tight lipped other than to say it wasn't much to do with the UK. At this, the other two gradually come to see that this was not much help to them. But the older man is ahead of them.

'Yeah, to you… I am…. useless, really,'

'And looks like I'm the slave' said the joiner.

'And I'm just the fool' joined the banker.

And then there was a long silence.

A history graduate has been listening to all this, across the aisle. She knows she really ought to understand all this, so she leans over and asked a really simple question:

'So, where do I fit in?'

The joiner asks if she was in work and she shyly confirms that she works in insolvency. Naturally, the banker asks her if the money was any good.

'Yes… for my boss; he charges me out at £100 per hour. I don't see a tenth of that, mind, so I can hardly cover the rent.'

The older man asks her about what her parents have.

'Dementia, mainly, and I am the main carer.'

'I wish I'd not asked'

Then there was a long public silence. And the train moved off.

THE NEXT GENERATION – THIS SHOULD BE YOUR TIME

So, we have discussed what we can do as individuals and as a nation. But, this update sets the analysis and messages in this book against one agenda only; that of the next generation. The aim of this chapter is to illustrate how the Mammonocracy pyramid favours one generation over another and may in time, divide those generations.

THE MAMMONOCRACY PYRAMID – ANOTHER VIEW

First, let's go back to the Mammonocracy pyramid and review what it is that we were grumbling about. A poor economic outlook in a world where we are poorly positioned to compete; a next generation, through no fault of their own, poorly placed to compete in the future; a divided and not a very happy society to grow up in. Remember August 2011. Let's look for some root causes. Yes, there was a brainless spree of criminality; but there was also a clear sense of rebellion by a group of people who sensed they were 'on the outside'. 'Outside' of what? Were they not 'on the outside' of the pyramid? Did they not destroy, in some part, symbols of our society because they felt, mistakenly or not, that they had no real stake or foothold in that society?

But, it is time to concentrate on the biggest issue facing UK plc in 2013; raising the next generation. Why? Quite apart from anything else, they will be in Government in a few years. They are the future. And they will have to fund our pensions.

So, where to start? You could start with the political system itself, but that is the subject of this book really. The point can be made by looking at five issues that should be most important to the young and where they should be the main drivers in policy discussions and where they should set priorities and policies.. There are plenty but let's pick just five areas of policy: Housing, Infrastructure, Education, Health, Opportunity; the next generation will all need housing, will all rely on services, will not compete if not educated, cannot afford poor health and will need the opportunity to make a start.

1. THE HOUSING CARTEL – THE ELEPHANT IN THE ROOM

Now, it is time for a new take on the high price of houses; it is a Bad Thing. Heresy, surely? Just go with us on this; like other things in this book it started with Mrs Thatcher. Councils were asked to sell their stock, so they stopped building, which increased private ownership, and generated more private wealth that enabled many to buy their own houses or to own multiple houses. Three ingredients for reduced supply. The demand has continued to go up and has become concentrated in certain areas, and as Mark Twain observed when advising others to buy land, no-one ain't making any more. There may have been no avowed intention to create a massive rise in prices; it just worked out rather well for those lucky enough to own property in desirable areas in the eighties. By the mid-eighties we were a Home Owning Democracy, which sounds respectable and aspirational; what we have since become is more like a Property Hoarding Cartel, and it is as horrid as it sounds. The average price of a house is now 5 or 6 times average earnings. Does this illustrate the strength of our economy? Not any more, it is an explanation for its weakness, because housing costs are a burden which the economy has to carry.

Of course, Government policy continues, largely, in conjunction with rising population, to fuel the crisis. We have low interest rates, law changes that favour landlords over tenants, and the latest lending proposals, all helping to maintain or even increase the size of the bubble. And the money men long since persuaded government to nationalise the problem, by buying dodgy banks; taxpayers are left with shares in busted banks which are reliant on property values to balance their books. And those who are outside the wealth control club, lose.

And the biggest losers, the next generation. When young people cannot afford accommodation near their work, how can they compete with Germans, Koreans or the Chinese? And it goes much deeper. When a graduate gets a job in London and lives 20 miles out she has huge transport costs. And when people pay for transport a big chunk of the costs is people costs, and a big chunk of that is the costs of their housing. And it goes wider: when people are forced to pay for parking, everywhere, even at hospital, they are paying into the coffers of the property cartel; when open spaces are sacrificed to developers, the profits go to the developers and the cost of rented property does not come down with it. When immigrants pay £350 a month to stay in unregulated outhouses in Outer London it is close to 'money for nothing' for unscrupulous landowners. And when our senior people are doing their level best to encourage younger folk to make the massive commitment to get a mortgage to 'get on the housing ladder' what they are really doing is asking the next generation to support the bubble from which they have derived such benefit already. Message to the next generation; be careful; you may not want to carry that burden around with you for the next 25 years, especially as the extent of that burden, interest, is controlled by, wait for it … bankers.

And what behaviours has the house price boom generated? In what direction has the housing market driven the economy? It has made a fortunate cohort relatively wealthy. It has encouraged a high level of personal debt. It has encouraged a significant spend on imports. And, in an age when competitive and flexible workforces are a necessity, it has created a situation where those who want to create wealth can hardly afford to live in places like London. So when the economy needs exports, lowering of debt and flexible labour, much of what the housing cartel achieves is precisely the opposite. Brilliant.

Now, how does this look to the next generation? Yes, they are beginning to work out that they are outside a club; and the anger will, justifiably, gather over time. To the next generation the housing cartel is a massive impediment to prosperity; it is becoming, to borrow a phrase, a tax on jobs. And more dangerously, it represents one generation's control over the next. What is the use of having one generation which is cash poor and property - rich and another that is, through no fault of its own, struggling to get work or start a career? The point is that, as in so many issues in this book, the money is there; it is in the wrong places and in the wrong hands. An intelligent government would seek to 'sweat the asset' that is our housing stock; the housing cartel serves mostly to waste it; in this way the housing market is a microcosm of the economy itself.

2. THE INFRASTRUCTURE ARGUMENT

One of the more hopeful signals from the current government has been the realisation of the value of infrastructure. Well done, but come on we have a lot of catching up to do. And there is a catch that the next generation need to be wise to. It is worth observing several ways in which the short – term advantages will have longer term costs for the next generation.

In the first place it is worth revisiting the discussion about PFI and its offshoots here. We talked of PFI being a mortgage. Who is paying and who is benefitting? Let's look at a hospital or school. As facilities are built there are benefits for the builders, the operators and the users of the facility; sound like the over 40's mostly. Who is paying? The Health Authorities, councils and other authorities. Yes, but their debt goes on for 30 or so years, does it not? So, most of that debt will get transferred to the next generation. But we don't recall them being asked for their opinion, do we? So, the magical sleight of hand that put PFI 'off-balance sheet' is, in reality a shoving of cost onto another generation. So, message to the under 30's; you have been set up, good and proper. And if someone did the same to the current lot, how long before they jump up and say 'can't pay, won't pay'. Already there are Health Authorities that cannot afford the staff to run their hospitals; it can only get worse. Now you know a bit more about why.

Another way of penalising the next generation was flagged a couple of years ago. Government signalled that it may have to review the way we pay for our roads. What this may mean is that roads will follow the water business and transfer to 'pay as you use'. This means tolls. And why is it significant? It means the next generation, notice the pattern, are taking much of the burden for today's' facility, the construction of which will generate turnover for today's generation. And because toll income is attractive, Government can sell the asset. So EDF own some of our electricity infrastructure and we can assume that the likes of Bouyges will take over some of our roads. Good for them but not so good for our next generation, who will look again at rail travel, where the fares have just gone up again by up to 9 percent.

There is another issue emerging about infrastructure. Maintenance budgets are being slashed; easy cuts to make. So the inheritance for the next generation is a network of pot-holed roads, patched up drainage. On behalf the next generation; thanks.

3. EDUCATION

There is one big horrible reason why politicians lose sight of the next generation. Why? They do not vote. But what did the UN say about the way we look after the next generation? Not good. They desperately need our investment, of time as well as money. And what does the tuition fees debate tell us? The next generation are soft targets. Easy money. To benefit who? Yes, the cohort who put us in the mess in the first place; no wonder 300,000 marched to protest about tuition fees in 2009. Our government want new entrants to the degree owners club to pay £30k to join the club; a club to which they were granted access for a third of that amount.

In this discussion education is much wider than visible, structured education; it is also about the education that occurs inside family life. Look at the next generation: if we are not interested in them now – when they need us – how interested will they be in us, later on, when we need them?

Mehr Zeit fur Kinder they say in Germany. Parenting should be the greatest labour of the greatest love. But in this country we see much too often the bawling child trying to attract the attention of parent sending a text or gazing into shops. And there are those busy people who proudly promise 'quality time' to their children, usually a few brief hours. The sad subtext here is that, for the rest of the time, the other 90% plus, the child is not the first priority. More sadly, the child knows it.

4. Health – the care crunch

A report in August 2012 indicated that one third of UK' primary school leavers are now clinically obese. Now, what has that got do with the economy? A great deal; to use a metaphor, those are the youngsters who are going to run, on our behalf, the next lap, in competition against the Chinese, Indians, Brazilians and the rest. Are they fit for the challenge? It doesn't sound good does it; obesity is linked to heart diseases, diabetes and, more recently discovered, asthma. So, how have we got here? Because, to continue the metaphor, their coaches – the current generation – chose to put up houses where once were playing fields. Because successive governments have been too heavily influenced by a food industry that makes the easiest of profits by turning us into a nation of over-eaters and sugar-obsessives. Just go into W H Smith for a paper and see if you can avoid the cut-price chocolate sales pitch; is this boosting retail or pushing drugs?

So, let's revisit the Care Crunch. Our productive people are increasingly stressed, our health system faces increasing demands arising from increasing numbers of aged people and our younger cohort are growing up increasingly prone to obesity, asthma and the rest. To borrow a phrase from the weather, we have the makings of a perfect storm.

5. Opportunities

We can start here with one compelling reason for investing in the next generation. Simply put, we can either spend now or we can spend later. Consider this, when the aid agencies go into a starvation zone, they much prefer to assist the victims to grow their own food and not rely on continuing supplies from outside. Now, interpret the metaphor: with nearly a quarter of our 18-25's jobless, that is close on a million victims, heading for dependency on the state funded equivalent of food parcels.

There is another way in which economic activity such as infrastructure investment is favouring the current generation over the next. Who is doing much of the work? Eastern Europeans and Indians running back offices. To whose benefit? The current generation, who benefit from the turnover and the facility at its newest. Who loses? A next generation of home grown personnel who will have reduced opportunity to gain the skills or experience to start a career.

THE BURDENED GENERATION

Now, go back to those 2011 riots, that whiff of unrest, that sense of a generation with little stake in society. Now, having read the paragraphs above, does it start to make sense? A bunch of 18 to 30's may not be able to fully articulate what it is that they are angry about, but they know instinctively that they are getting a rough deal. It is not even as if we are saying that there is some sort of evil masterplan. But there is a pattern under which the ruling class – the Mammonocracy Generation – are building the safeguards for their relatively comfortable future by taking advantage of those – the Burdened Generation - who have limited leverage with which to oppose. Is it fair? You decide.

WHAT TO WISH FOR

Is it all doom and gloom? Well, not entirely. Actually, this should be one of the more cheering paragraphs in the book. We all now know how much unnecessary money is going into Wealth Control and how much unnecessary work goes on in Management Support. We can still see ways of improving efficiency of the productive class and reducing the burden of dependants. We can see the risk of a generational divide. We remain a nation full of ideas, energy and knowledge. So, if we cut the waste in the top two layers, pursue efficiency in the other two, and watch the generation divide there ought to be enough for us to continue doing most of things that we really, really want or need to do. Wahoo! How good is that? Bring it on.

But... and here's the rub, we cannot wait. We need a politician who has the courage, toughness and independence of spirit to attack the wastes within the Mammonocracy pyramid and to address the generational divide that is inherent in it. The search starts here. And why does it matter? Be absolutely certain about this, if the next generation are not engaged and Government policy continues to address the demands of, say, an ageing third of the population, we are in deep trouble; be very worried about the disenfranchised two thirds or a 'Burdened Generation' if adjustment is not made. History teaches us how quickly events can turn, say, if international markets start to doubt our capacity to repay those debts; how quickly interest rates, on both public and private debt, can double; how quickly the Day of the Vultures dawns, with the loss of liquidity and the fire sales of assets. The events of August 2011 were a brutal warning of the undercurrents at home; the scenes from Greece and Cyprus serve as warnings from abroad.

SOME PERSPECTIVE

And some final comments. As has been said before: be thankful for a great deal that is good. There are millions of people in the rest of the world who are dying – some literally – to be here in Britain. The Olympics showed that this is still a country that has a huge amount going for it. The risk of following Greece, Cyprus, Ireland or Iceland is real but we have the opportunity to dodge that outcome. All that money scarcely made us happier, so, how about a slightly fairer society, even if there are those who have a little less? To sum it up, go back to the quote at the head of Chapter 6 'what is important to people is to be able to do and be'. You cannot say fairer than that.

So, set worry aside, for now.... and go out and do something randomly kind.

BIBLIOGRAPHY

Atkinson, Dan and Elliot, Larry, *Fantasy Island*
Constable, London, 2007

Blanchard PhD, Ken and Johnson MD, Spencer, *The One Minute Manager*
    HarperCollins, London, 2004

Boswell and Johnson, *To the Hebrides: Samuel Johnson's Journey to the Western Islands and James Boswell's Journal of a Tour*
    Birlinn Ltd, Edinburgh, 2007

Brown, Hamish, *Hamish's Groats End Walk*
    Paladin, London, 1983

Bunting, Madeleine, *Willing Slaves*
    HarperCollins, London, 2004

Cable, Vince, *The Storm*, Atlantic Books
    London, 2009

Craig, David and Elliott, Matthew, *Fleeced*, Constable London, 2009

Crane, Nicholas, *Two Degrees West*
    Penguin, London, 2000

Dorling, Daniel, *Fair Play*
    Hodder and Stoughton, London 2011

Forrester, Vivianne, *The Economic Horror*
    Polity Press, Cambridge, 1999

Gladwell, Malcolm, *Outliers*
Penguin, London, 2008

Holy Bible, New International Version
    Hodder & Stoughton, London, 1979

Hutton, Will, *The State We're In*
    Vintage, London, 1995

Kemp, Gill, *Talking Families, Talking Communities* Childline/Calor Gas, London, 2005

King, Anthony and Crewe, Ivor, *The Blunders of our Governments*, Oneworld, London, 2013

Lansley, Stewart, *Rich Britain*
    Politico's, London, 2006

Lowe, Steve and McArthur, Alan, *Is It Just Me or Is Everything Shit?*
    Sphere Books, London, 2005

Machiavelli, Niccolo, *The Prince*
    Oxford University Press, New Ed edition, 2005

O'Harrow, Robert, *No Place To Hide*
    The Free Press, USA, 2005

Orwell, George, *1984*
    Secker and Warburg, London, 1949

Peston, Robert, *Who Runs Britain?*
    Hodder and Stoughton, London, 2008

Stiglitz, Joseph, *Globalization and its Discontents*
    Penguin, London, 2002

Toynbee, Polly and Walker, David, *Did Things Get Better?* Penguin,
    London, 2001

Wilkinson, Richard and Pickett, Kate, *The Spirit Level*
    Penguin, London, 2009

ADDITIONAL SOURCES

Atkins Group plc, Annual Report, 2006

BT plc, Annual Report, 2007

Carillion plc, Annual Report, 2006

Census 2001, HMSO, London, 2002

Childline, www.childline.org.uk, website, current

Confederation of British Industry, www.cbi.org.uk, website, current

Competition Commission, Groceries Market Investigation, Final Report, Competition Commission, London, 2008

Help The Aged, www.helptheaged.org.uk, website, current

HM Treasury, Pre-Budget Statement 2007, Comprehensive Spending Review, London, 2007

House of Commons Transport Committee, The London Underground and the Public-Private Partnership Agreements, Second Report of Session 2007–8

House of Commons Public Accounts Committee, Tendering and Benchmarking in PFI, Sixty-third Report of Session, 2006–7

Institute of Chartered Accountants, England and Wales (ICAEW), Career Benchmarking Survey 2007, ICAEW, London, 2007

Institute for Public Policy Research (Robinson, Hawksworth, Broadbent, Laughlin, Haslam), 'The Private Finance Initiative – Saviour, Villain or Irrelevance?', IPPR, London

Joseph Rowntree Foundation, www.jrf.org.uk, website, current

nfpSynergy/Samaritans, 'Stressed Out: a study of public experience of stress at work', Samaritans, London, 2007

Office for National Statistics, Census, 2001

Orton, Michael and Rowlingson, Karen, 'Public Attitudes to Economic Inequality', Joseph Rowntree Foundation, York

Samaritans, www.samaritans.org, website, current

Shelter, www.shelter.org.uk, website, current

UNICEF Innocenti Research Centre, 'An overview of child well-being in rich countries', UNICEF, Florence, 2007

Westwood, Andy, 'Not Very Qualified', The Work Foundation, London, 2001

We Are What We Do, www.wearewhatwedo.org, website, current

National Child Measurement Programme, 2012/13, Report and Data.

Marylebone Cricket Club, 'Chance to Shine', April 2013, report of findings by Opinion Matters

Suggested Further Reading

Bausch, Randy, *Last Lecture*, Hyperion (US), Hodder & Stoughton (UK)

Field, Lynda, *60 Ways to Change your Life*, Element Books, England

Grieve, Bradley Trevor, The *Book for People Who Do Too Much*, Andrew McMeel Publishers, Kansas, USA

Johnson, Spencer, *One Minute for Yourself*, R Collins Paperbacks

We Are What We Do, *Change the World for a Fiver*, We Are What We Do, London, via website wearewhatwedo.org

We Are What We Do, *Change the World from 9 to 5*, We Are What We Do, London, via website wearewhatwedo.org

Wilson, Paul, *The Little Book Of Calm*, Penguin, London